Passion & Pain

by JJ Johnson

Passion & Pain

Printed in the United States of America.

ISBN: 0615503942
ISBN-13: 978-0615503943

Library of Congress Control Number: 2011911189
Publisher: Seeds and Weeds Publishing
Schenectady, NY

Additional copies of this book may be purchased through:
createspace.com
Createspace an Amazon.com Company
and
amazon.com

Also available at
www.passion-and-pain.com or
www.seeds-and-weeds.com/passion-and-pain.html

Dedication

For all the inspirations
Lori & BB
SQ
Lisa
BJ
Maggie
Heather
AH
Jen
RR
Michele
Robin
DF
SC
Kathy
Cathy
Cookie
Laura
Rae
Fawnia
JD
AD
JB
KB
CAA
Chris
Christy
the DreamM QTz
the Kimwood girls

Steve, you were real, the madness was not.

CAVEAT

Passion & Pain, unlike the preceding Seeds & Weeds, delves into the shadow and uncertainty of melancholy. The topics of obsession, sex and suicide are prominent throughout. I do not recommend reading it if these concepts offend or disturb you. Some of the language and subject matter is graphic and definitely not for children. The fact that these are issues I have dealt with throughout my life is the very reason for writing these poems. Sometimes the only way to get through the difficult times, for me, has been writing poems and looking from the outside in to gain a new perspective. I didn't write them as therapy, but they have had just that affect on me. I could ask if I should hide them away and not allow anyone to read them, but it seems to me that would be copping out or pretending a part of me doesn't exist.

In addition to the darkness, there is also love and affection entangled within. I hope that some will read these poems and relate to the feelings expressed in them. For that reason alone, they are worth putting into this collection. Many of these poems were written for people who have deeply touched my life, sometimes in a positive way, but more often, not for the better. I hope the inclusion of any of these poems does not harm the hearts of anyone in any way. They are a part of me and I am not afraid to expose my dark side.

What I hope to accomplish with this collection of poems is to debunk the misperception by some that I am always a nice guy who never does anything wrong. I may be to blame for creating this myth in the first place. While I am a nice guy and try to follow the concept that nice guys don't finish last, we just want to be sure no one gets left behind, I often fall short of my own expectations. I am just as vulnerable to the weeds in 3 Seeds as anyone else. They have held me back time and time again in life and I must do better.

Chapter 1: **Back To The Egg**

Chapter 2: **Broken Bonds**

Chapter 3: **Interlude**

Chapter 4: **Innerlewd**

Chapter 5: **Lust**

Chapter 6: **Seven-Year Obsession**

Chapter 7: **The Point**

Chapter 8: **Veiled In Shadow**

Chapter 9: **The Dream Is Over**

Chapter 10: **The Recurring Curse**

Chapter 11: **After the Fall**

Chapter 12: **Knight Fall**

Chapter 13: **Maggie-Margret & Heather**

Chapter 14: **Empty Nest**

Chapter 15: **The Darkives**

Chapter 16 contains bonus poems not included in the original printing of Passion & Pain, written after the first edition was published.
This revision was completed in November 2014.

CAVEAT:
Many of these poems are of an erotic or dark nature.

Chapter 16: **Bonus Poems**

Passion & Pain

By JJ Johnson

Chapter 1: Back To The Egg

01: Back To The Egg: 03/25/1982

02: Descent: 02/28/2007

03: Surrender the Phantom: 04/20/2010

04: A Grave Half-Empty: 02/14/2007

05: Unloved Alone But She Loved Him: 02/25/2009

06: Eleven Years Road By: 10/01/2009

07: Goodbye Mr. Bear: 04/20/2010

08: The Fool That Never Knowed: 01/11/2011

09: Traitor in Our Midst: 01/01/2010

10: Hey Joe, What Does It Mean If It Burns When I Piss?: 07/05/1990

11: If Closets Could Talk: 07/06/1990

Back to the Egg

Good-bye my friend
I'm goin' back to the egg
Where no light ever shines
To the void of the mind
Leavin' life far behind
Yes my ship will be sailing tomorrow

Good-bye my dear
I'm goin' back to the egg
Where no one's ever been
So that I can't be seen
While I lie back and dream
Yes my dear I'll be dreaming about you

Leaving on that dirt road down there
'Cos you don't seem to care
And you've got them lying for you
But babe who's lyin' on you
Has he eyes enough to see through your smile?

Good-bye my love
I'm goin' back to the egg
Going to lie down and sleep
In the womb of the Earth
Back before my life's birth
Yes my love I'll be sleeping tomorrow

Descent

I clearly saw the fog descending on the city
Depositing a film of condensation, like pity
Dripping from the awning, her tears drew rivers
Cleansing the morning of the sun's rising slivers
Forming a path towards the past she can't escape
Forgotten in words, drawn without shape
The sky grew blue behind the gray phantom
Clarity blew the mind of the blue-eyed one at random
Precisely when ordered in a timely fashion
Expectations demanded she dressed well for passion
Though she never expected his figure to float
Surrounding her flesh with the words that he wrote
His verse carried waves rolling patterns in wet sand
The dew covered beach lost the battle for dry land

Surrender the Phantom

Wait, wait a day, again, one more, eternal Déjà Vu
Change but the angle of motionless shadows

Seasons rise and fall in circular sacrifice to sparring gods
What god survives to observe the surrender to this ache?

Defenseless to conclude the assault of perpetuity
What secret waits to release the haunting apparition?

The reeking mist of decay concealed beneath still living flesh
Long since departed, the specter flaunts his camouflage

The pointless ruse is pointed out from within its beating heart
Beaten into silence by a spirit existing in the past

A past when hope held the hand of one that held life with piety
But all a dream is all it was, a mere phantom dies in misery

A Grave Half-Empty

You can't imagine my pain
A ladder to infinite loneliness
Rungs break one by one with each step
As the depths rise up around this grave
With no death to fill it's hollowed ground
No corpse to fowl the sweet scent of desire
No flowers adorn the unknown site
Where unborn love grows beyond the rim of darkness
While insecurity feeds tireless shovels
Soiling the ground I look up to
Piling higher toward a suffocating collapse
I would fill my lungs with each choking handful
Dropped from the fingers of lovers never touched
Felt only in the heart of one ever undesired
The one whose love lives on, unknown and alone
Whose grave rests in pieces
Pieced together by hands too dirty to hold
Held back by a heart afraid of the dark
Imprisoned by shackles it can't envision
And you can't imagine

Unloved Alone But She Loved Him

He was loved but did not know
Would not allow the sight to see
Could not let go of fear to lose
Tried not to fall when tripped his shadow
Turned his back when faced with her
To see she was behind him all along
Redness filled his eyes with tears
Showing clarity beneath her flowing veil
For all he would be is nothing more and nothing less
Than the emptiness a heart unloved and loved
Can touch another without knowing in denial
She confessed to all, that he is blind
He could not feel what was never learned
Knowing for sure he was unloved, he knew, he knew
Not knowing how, unwilling to let go of pain
Denying pain blinder than love, he was loved
Seized the pain, love fell empty, felt alone
In stillness the flowing veil flew to him
Exposing secrets long since elapsed
When he was certain he was unloved
But was loved, was loved, was loved

Eleven Years Road By

One day eleven years from now
I saw you sitting at the table in the shop
A Dunkin' Donut sat next to you
as you gazed at the empty chair
Smiling at the sight of me you couldn't see was there
Though I was behind you,
close enough to touch your hair
I'm sorry for leaving you,
we both know life is so unfair

Did you buy the Apple Crumb for me
Hoping somehow I would lift it in the air?
Even if you could see me here
you could do no more than stair
For ghosts are merely specters that live in the nowhere
Perhaps I might be there with you
if I had taken better care
But how could I know I would finally find love
in one so pure and fair?

For now I look in each bus window
That rides past your empty seat
Watching to see your face
searching for my smile
Eleven years road by in just a little while
I knew you would return one day
to release your hearts denial
To be set free of your guilty plea
in a never ending trial

Goodbye Mr. Bear

Tonight, Mr. Bear is layin' next to me
I wonder if he's thinkin' about you, the way that I do
To hold you in his arms, is a distant wish come true
He must be wonderin' if he'll ever lay with you

Each night, Mr. Bear sleeps in our bed
He whispers in my ear, all the things I wish you said
I hold him in my arms, but my aching heart feels dead
We both keep wonderin' who lays with you instead

Good morning Mr. Bear, it's time for you to wake
You can't just lay there in a bed you didn't make
She's comin' back for you and the things she didn't take
Don't be nervous lil one, my son, no need for you to shake
Your heart is the only one that she cannot break

The Fool That Never Knowed

Sometimes it's hard to tell
the difference between
what's real and what's pretend
Did you mean to flee the scene?

Was I just an accident
waiting for you to happen on me
Did you mean to spend the rent
when I told you love is free?

You promised me so many things
Not one was ever true
I'm always the fool who believes
what I would not do to you

It was supposed to be forever
From the day I shared your vow
Now our story of love is over
So what do I do now?

It all seems so ridiculous
I can't pretend to know
This road don't lead back to us
I don't know where to go

Walking again the same old road
Was paved for the likes of me
with the gold of fools that never knowed
that nothing's ever free

Traitor in Our Midst

Inexorably I had prepared for our bond
Risked everything I waited patiently
Years I dreamed my waking days away
For the dreams to come only while sleeping

Twenty years is only a marker in time
Five more a friendship is marked for death
Nearly two more than life had blessed you with
There was not enough in all the universe

How can such bright sunlight cast no shadows?
So blinded was eye that I could not see
Hidden in plain sight on a plane over my head
And you slipped behind the shadow he did not leave

Knowing twenty winters I endured cast away
Knowing my island charts were torn in a storm
Knowing I would not be home on Christmas day
Knowing you would be, the traitors knife sunk in

Hey Joe, What Does It Mean If It Burns When I Piss?

I covered for your lies `cos I was your friend
You claim it was only every now and then
Seems more like every now and every then
In fact there's no time I can't remember when

Remember the night after her party
The night you transformed me from a friend into a tool
When you drove the bodacious one out behind the school
You never saw it coming but caught her tainted jewel

Now I fear that even truth can't set me free
I don't want to hurt her again when she's my friend too
She'd leave you and despise me if she only knew
I went along when I knew all along it wasn't true

As if date rape wasn't bad enough for her
You made her pay your doctor's bills for giving you herpes
Made her feel false guilt and bare your burden on her knees
For turning her true love into a sexual disease

She has suffered so, imagine how she felt
Believing it was her fault for making your dick melt
When all along it was your cheating with her best friend
You are the virus that brought four friendships to an end

If Closets Could Talk

When friendship's based on lies
The truth can remain hidden but it never dies
It lives and breeds within, consuming hope for peace of mind
Will my avowal allow me to seek what I must find?

You are not worthy of her
And she deserved so much more than you ever were
I'd have given anything to touch her kind of love
I wonder, do you care who you're under or above?

Wuz we best friends back then?
Now I'm ashamed when I look back at were we've been
I'd have done it differently if I had lived your life
Love was not enough, you could have had the perfect wife

I'm through lying for you
Dusting off old skeletons so they match the new
I realized too late that you never were my friend
And I'm left to carry a pain that will not mend

Our friendship's based on lies
And my guilt tares me apart every time she cries
But still I cannot tell her for fear she'll hate me too
The truth won't help me now, I'm damned no matter what I do

Now that's unimportant
To cause so much pain was the inverse of my intent
It matters not that I am not the only one to blame
I still bear the guilt for extinguishing the flame

Chapter 2: Broken Bonds

12: Soul Silhouette: 08/31/2003

13: Where Are You Going?: 04/16/1984

14: At The End Of Every Rainbow: 07/01/1988

15: Sometimes Wishes Come True: 01/01/2003

16: Eye Of The Pirate, Heart Of A Thief: 03/25/2001

17: The Act No One Wants To See: 06/13/2010

18: Trap-Eas-y-To-Fall-In-Two: 08/17/2004

19: A Door Too Close To Closed To Adore You: 05/11/2005

20: Swing Set: 07/22/1999

21: What Happened To Us?: 10/26/1989

22: Drive Home: 12/31/1987

Soul Silhouette

Forgive and forget
Is a phrase I have used
You're certain you've won some twisted bet
But I'm afraid you have the facts confused
And you shouldn't count the payout yet
For trust isn't something to be abused
No my trust isn't something you should have abused

There is no regret
To be found within you
Wealth is all you know how to pursue
Though money can never repay your debt
So give from within, your payment's past due
Learn to stand tall without a safety net
It's time you were more than a dark silhouette

Where Are You Going? I've Seen Where You've Been!

Where are you going and where have you been?
You've learned nothing at all from all that you've seen
You don't care who you hurt, you don't know what love means
Ain't it funny how life never is as it seems?

You've been hurt and now you ignore the pain
So many times you think you're going insane
There's no way to stop it now, no end to your game
And one day you'll know there's no one else you can blame

With all of your lies and the way that you flew
It's hard to believe you're the girl that I knew
With the life that you've led and with all you've been through
Did you ever wonder what'll become of you?

My fine feathered lover, watch out, beware
Your flight path is less a circle than a square
You've turned all the sharpest corners and cut them all clean
Tell me, where are you going and where have you been?

Where Are You Going? I've Seen Where You've Been! *(continued)*

You used to be such an innocent girl
Your beauty once shined like the whitest of pearls
You love to get sun-tanned while laying on the lawn
But now it is raining and your color's all gone

You'll find yourself living out in the street
Then a pimp will find you and you'll kiss his feet
He'll use you and sell you till you're no good anymore
Then you'll realize what you've become is a whore

Where are you going? I've seen where you've been
Now you've spread your legs and let them all in
Do you know what you're doing? I think it's a sin
But you'll keep on doing it again and again

You dance around like a sweet high class queen
You're sleeping habits are completely obscene
Burning your sheets has become a daily routine
I wonder where you're going, I've seen where you've been

At The End Of Every Rainbow

Rainbows rise from a pot of gold
And fall at the end of a lonely road

When speaking of love the story's retold

For what gave it strength
So often gets sold

While betrayal is hidden behind a blindfold

Sometimes Wishes Come True

Sometimes wishes come true but not in times like these
It won't help me to beg you and get down on my knees
There's no birthday candles or magic lanterns to rub
I'd have more luck with leprechauns in St Patrick's Pub

You're the only one who can make this one come true
I don't know black magic from white, but it's made me blue
You're a charming sorceress with a potion inside your heart
Your witchcraft has left me breathless and falling apart

Had I known your spell was just a trick of the mind
Could I have cast it out before falling left me blind?
I didn't realize fooling my heart was all a stratagem
Sometimes wishes come true but this is not one of them

Eye Of The Pirate, Heart Of A Thief

Your hull is breached by pirates at sea
Robbing your treasure and slipping away
Faces behind masks and eyes you can't see
Denying your pleasure, you wish they would stay

For in spite of the pain, something inside
Makes the wish to set sail into the waves
Pass through your lips like questions unasked
The answers are found in watery graves

For the waves would overcome us both
Out of control and going down fast
There is barely time to take a breath
Wondering how long our air supply will last

If only I could be there with you
No questions would ever cross our lips
We would already have the answers
Setting the courses for two colliding ships

The Act No One Wants To See

Holding you as close as flesh can embrace
felt three dimensions apart
Now I feel more than my empty hands
have sensed when clenched in rage
I wasn't satisfied with the rations
that twenty years of hunger fed me
The overflow from your heart
I devalued through one-dimensional desire
Evidently I am more lost
than when you found me wandering naked and alone
Exposing the veil of darkness
layered over hidden scars not meant to be seen
I showed them to you hoping to seem
more human than the ghost of my past
Pride is a shadow sewn to cloak all
I have tried to hide from attractive spectators
I am every bit the bit player in a cast of characters
I push on an overcrowded stage
Failing the audition is to be expected
by an extra, leading without direction
Reading the script through stains on torn skins
the lamb smugly rose above
Lowering my head in humility
when no one is looking at the player I've become
Smashing the mirror that begs me to look
into the eyes of blind honesty
Only to reveal there is no one
looking back from the fractured shards
How pleasing their edge would be to cut through
the act no one wants to see

Trap-Eas-y-To-Fall-In-Two

It would appear that thoughts of me
do not cross the pathways of your mind
Nearly so often as those of you
swing from one wire to another in mine

Once again the natural state of my fate
reaches its smothering arms around me
Crushing the fantasy my heart creates
over and over setting your fleeting heart free

The relationship you seek I regret
Is as painful to me as my love is to you
So please just forget we ever met
Let memories of me fade away from your view

A Door Too Close To Closed To Adore You

It could have been, what would have been?
Trust now lost behind a door too far away
The knob too far to reach is still unseen
Without reasons to cum, no reason to stay

Yet you were everything in every dream
Red hair that made my heart reflect its flame
The ones that cum are never all they seem
And who is left alone is who is left to blame

Why then does this empty heart seek infinity
Never ending pain with no beginning found
Closed the door and there stood Serendipity
Her foot jammed before it slammed, I heard her pleasing sound

Don't listen to the siren sing her fatal song
Push harder, close the gap, break her God damn foot
Love is just a waste of time, as far as time is long
And if her toes fall off, remember, next time wear a boot

Swing Set

Your smile is hard but sensual
Your striking eyes test all that's visual
Your blazing hair flows like wisps of fire
And I feel myself rise a little higher

There is a sharpness inside you
I would love to soften yet not subdue
Relax your mind, feel my mental massage
Open your heart and remove your camouflage

There was one thing holding me back
Now my heart has found the courage I lack
For I have felt since the first time we met
That the two of us would make a perfect set

I wouldn't dare pass up this chance
You've turned me on to this wild way of dance
I wanna fly, so let's get down and swing
To be with you I would try most anything

What Happened To Us?

Neither one of us cheated
Neither one of us lied
We both got what we wanted
But now we're both empty inside

Well honey I wanna know
What happened to us?
We thought our love would grow
Who could predict that it would bust?

Did we take it in to fast?
How could the well run dry?
Now our love is in the past
And neither one of us knows why

We shared all of our secrets
We shard our dreams and trust
Our passion's gone but owes no debts
Tell me now what happened to us?

Love and sex walked hand in hand
We loved it soft or rough
We gave it all we had
Maybe we didn't take enough

We could give it one more try
But we won't answer the call
When I stop to wonder why
Maybe it wasn't love at all

Drive Home

Drive Home
Johnny won't you drive on home?
And when you're on your way away from here
Why don't you tilt back and down a beer?
Drive Home!

Drive home
Johnny don't you drive alone
There is no need to fear what you can't see
So relax and have a beer on me
Drive Home!

Drive home
Johnny got your friend all stoned
He says "Beware of that telephone pole"
The faster you speed the more heads will roll
Drive Home!

Drive home
Johnny you won't make it home
A fair price to pay is the fate you'll share
Tonight's the night you're gonna lose your hair
Drive Home!

Drive Home
Johnnies mother's on the phone
Johnnies friend won't be sleeping in his bed
It rolled so far they haven't found his head
Fly Home!

Fly Home
Johnny sings the jailbird moan
You felt lucky cause you survived the ride
But locked in your cell you can't run and hide
You're Home!

Chapter 3: **Interlude**

23: Bar Fly: 08/12/1989

24: Expose Yourself: 09/25/1991

25: Beyond the Mask: 03/16/2001

26: In the Sky There Is No Limit: 06/28/2001

27: Intercourse of Hearts: 02/14/2006

28: Mutual Attraction: 07/21/1984

29: Lost and Found: 08/01/2000

30: Naked Passion: 06/9-06/12/2006

Bar Fly

You'd think it was heaven
The way you fly to the bar
To be with your boyfriend
He wants to be a rock star

When you're a woman (barfly, barfly)
Watch out where you go
Men don't care why (barfly, barfly)
It's what you can do
It ain't who you know

You look great in this light
And I have only had two
Someone started a fight
He saw them lookin' at you

I want to tell you (barfly, barfly)
Fly over my way
You know what to do (barfly, barfly)
Can I buy you a drink?
'Cos I want to play!

Do you know how it feels?
Do ya wanna take a chance?
Baby take off those heels
C'mon let's get down and dance

You shake it so well (barfly, barfly)
Get closer to me
We might go to hell (barfly, barfly)
Well I'm on my way
Will you cum with me?

Expose Yourself

Taking tips to show what's under your pants
Is not a ladies way to dance
I see through this game you play
And I don't want to see you that way

As your friend I'll offer some advice
Find yourself or you may pay a price
Losing who you used to be
Also amounts to losing me

You like giving men a mental boff
Is that your way of getting off?
But I know what's underneath
A broken heart lies hidden beneath

You've donned the mask he wants you to wear
But it's too late now, he doesn't care
Expose yourself but that's the wrong part
You need only uncover your heart

Beyond The Mask

What ya want from me, ya wanna see my kitty?
Did you wanna pay in cash to tell me I look pretty?
And if I do a dance while I'm sittin' on your lap
Do ya care if I think you're just
another heartless, lonesome sap?

If you really want to know, I do it for the money
But no matter how big the bill, you'll never taste my honey
I'll only give you what I want, so don't bother to even ask
I will never let you see
the tears beneath this kitty mask

I've got a job to do and lots of bills at home to pay
And I won't come home with you no matter what you say
So look at me, desire me, then go home and please yourself
But before you go out the door,
don't forget to share the wealth

(Inspired through interview with Fawnia Mondey Dietrich)

In The Sky There Is No Limit

Seeing them every time,
always looking up at the sky
They seem to be praying to meet
a goddess eye to eye
Gazing and waiting at the alter
for an answer from heaven
Faithful in their offerings, hoping for one of the seven

The disciples with little,
are still willing to give it
Feeling so divine,
for in the sky there is no limit
The touch of two eyes contacting
the hope reaching out from theirs
They need the coveted smile to complete their passionate stairs

Teasing their desires
makes them want for even more
Showing them just a little
of what they hunger for
Stoking the fire, then backing off
the flames till each one begs
To see what the little kitty has nestled between her legs

Each night they are in awe
of the moon up in the sky
Feeling free to dance on the clouds
which drift from eye to eye
Knowing just when the time is right
to give them what they come for
But never pet the kitty, petters get bounced out of the door

(Inspiration from Fawnia Mondey Dietrich)

Intercourse of Hearts

Passion's beat is no less real
than if we had spoken silent verse
The flesh is superficial
and my heart does not have sex
It feels what it feels
based on its own criteria
Remaining hidden from my mind
for reasons still unfathomable
I'll not penetrate flesh 'til we've shared
the intercourse of hearts
To correspond our feelings without words
in amorous embrace
Only then to be content with the pleasure
of intimate exchange
In mind and heart with body and soul
to hear this thunder roll
I crave this more
than all I have thirsted for in life
Now all I require is a muse
to consummate the music we create

Mutual Attraction

We've got a mutual attraction
With desires we try to satisfy
But I don't want that kind of action
Cause when true love is missing, so am I

The curves you move cause me distraction
When I touch your sensitive silky thigh
I feel your natural cuntraction
But when your love is missing, so am I

You fuel my fire with your lust potion
But girl I know how it feels to get high
There's no substitute for emotion
And when my love is missing, so am I

We share a mutual attraction
With desires we'll never satisfy
But we don't need that kind of action
So if our love is missing, so am I

Lost and Found

All around me I sensed
Dimensions unexplored
A feeling so real I could not have ignored
It must have been fate that touched me
And guided my hands
Across my keyboard

When all seemed to be lost
Without corporal trace
Destiny led me to the right time and place
Yet it was you who made it real
That opened my heart
Through love with grace

Amorous force escorts me
Through endless cyber space
Opening all eyes to this hidden place
Where two lost souls become found as one
Sharing desires
Without seeing a face

Nothing seemed clear to me
When we met at the start
Echoes of unheard whispers kept us apart
But a voice from inside enticed me
To listen and hear
The truth in my heart

Naked Passion

I await your next sentence
Before another can be written
Checking my inbox, pressing refresh
Clicking the link, watching for passion
My fingers type with restless hands bound behind me
As if in two places at once but neither where I want
To place them on you, to feel your nakedness
In the palm of my hand, on the tip of my tongue
The thoughts you invoke, the words you inspire
I am lost in your mind and found in your heart
My passion rises as you tease me to new heights
Pointing me in a direction of a beach called paradise
Guiding with your hand, driving through your forest
Leaping from the edge to swim inside your pool
My body tingles from the thought of loving you
It's all so real when you tell me of your touch
I can feel every circle and stroke you send to me
Somehow your fingers have entered my forbidden mind
You've reached out to caress, to hold, to feel
While your lips kiss, and lick, you taste and swirl
My goddess, you have me on fire, ready to erupt
But holding back to make it last a little longer
And I am powerless to reach the climax
Until you decide to make my nectar cum
Will you taste me or place me inside your paradise?
Will you give me one more stroke or mount your lover's ride?

Chapter 4: **Innerlewd**

31: Shadow and Bone: 02/22/2011

32: Reckless Fire: 08/28/2003

33: The Forest or The Trees?: 06/09/2000

34: Of Feathers and Fantasy: 03/28/2011

35: Crescent Blu Moon: 04/01/2011

36: Fair Lucy St. Anne: 06/09/2010

37: As A Matter of Fact or Fiction: 12/04/1989

38: Just Say Yes: 06/24/2001

39: The Difference Between Night And Day: 12/21/1987

40: Fantasy Lovers: 11/01/1983

Shadow and Bone

will you steal time with me
or just seduce and fuck me secretly?
do you live your own stereotype
or just imitate the shadows you wish were your own?

if the world expanded
no further than your welcome matted door
who would call from beyond the wood
that swings open to expose a barricade of bricks

who would come to knock it down
when the mortar dried between stones held far enough apart?
their similarities will never touch
squeezed secretly behind the wood where shadows cast unseen

take a walk where no path leads
drop the glare that guards your secrets from me
unconfined jewels mingle loosely
under the lid of the box with locks protecting them

all that lies between our love
un-solid darkness seen by all who witness light
unseen clarity hides a hard hearts cage
until exposure proves forever is too late

Reckless Fire

Lost words are more than merely echoes in my mind
A poem dies on paper, you may as well be blind
Still ears want to vibrate with each beat of your heart
Like a thunderous crescendo aching for the start

Waiting in anticipation for reality
The hunger to feast on love or to be set free
To consume what little within remains alive
This craving drives up higher with its will to thrive

All the yesterdays past by, without a taken chance
Carefree or careless, it's high time to drop these pants
Disregarding consequences no matter how dire
Reckless desire yields to its need for feminine fire

The Forest or the Trees?

Anywhere, Anyplace, Anytime
Licentious souls combine
Craving to compose
A visual poem of unheard verse

In throws of passion merging their wish
The forest conceals the fetish
Creating one song
Drawn risqué lyrics to which two belong

Yet it's what can't be seen by open eyes
Silence to all ears
Carving howls into the wood
Making love, the art of hidden display

Of Feathers and Fantasy

tickle me tenderly tonight
when I fall asleep so deep
wrap yourself around my heart
tie me to your sultry soul
bind my hands behind your back
and yours around my neck
don't let me take, don't let me fake
make me submit to your fiery will
your fingers feather touch will tease
and if you please turn them round
to sharply show you're in control
of my bleeding and my pain
knowing that the time will cum
when pleasure cries the rain
when thunder cracks its whip
four stampeding legs ablaze
ten claws embrace one curvature
the race creates a lions roar
as climax escapes its broken cage
two fantasies collapse
if king and queen fall to dream
which one will rise to reign?

Crescent Blu Moon

are you naught but a shadow on a misty spring morning
vanishing and reappearing with the blowing wind?
when I open my eyes a breeze fools my senses
making me wonder were you a memory or dream
but for the scent of passion that soaked into my thoughts
and scratches concealed may be imagined or real
the candle I relight discloses where you hide
the flame vanquished each time you pass over me
making warm flesh tingle when darkness hides two lovers
evening storms with thunder as seeds shower new life
under crescent blu moons with pink sky delights
a sensual vapor caresses as it crosses my skin
condensation flows a river deep within
till dawns eruptions steal riches from the pour
quenching their thirst as a journey begins
while sprouting wings arch into the violate air

Fair Lucy St. Anne

Oh Lucy fair Lucy
You tempt me, you tease me
Temporarily please me
Then make me forget how to smile

Together I share your solitary gaze
Luring me with an allure that stings
What else can I do as you coax me to care?
When you said that you loved me last night

The sun rise disturbed this morning's walk
Holding your hand I wandered alone
Awaiting the cold that burned my will
Your fire was not of the sky

And Lucy, fair Lucy
Enticed me this morning to rise
Once more to taunt, once more she smiled
I freely resolve to comply

As A Matter of Fact or Fiction

My love swirls ‘round the toilet bowl
Within a ribbed prison of latex control
Because you don’t want more hungry offspring
And I’m not keen to catch your fiery sting

But the loneliness of abstinence
Is crushing twice once common sense
Taking refuge in our convenient exchange
Knowing the shot confined falls out of range

Exhaustion finds us both asleep
And morning blinds the time we keep
The day drags on with unending guilt
For desires to fill them with more passion spilt

To flush each thought of mistaken love
Masking the feeling, snuggly wrapped in a glove
In desperation we meet again
Yet now is not our time to question when

Just do the deed and then be done
When together we are concerned with only one
Still, one in the company of one more
Is less lonely than hands two less than four

Just Say Yes

To say the very least
You are pleasing to the eyes
And I wonder if you would be
Just as pleasing to my rise

But at the very least
You have given me a smile
Now I wonder if we could love
Just for a little while

We have the very least
But will give and take it all
It's no wonder covered lovers
Impeding garments fall

And in the very least
You will be one with my flesh
You may wonder where I have been
All your life, Just say Yes

The Difference Between Night And Day

Hypnotized by a vision seen
A lipstick smile; sharp and wicked mean
Dark shadowed gaze connects eye to eye
Lips teasing an unspoken lie

Amorous scent blown through the air
Made cold broken hearts burn with desire
Ever hoping to satisfy her
Ever failing to satisfy her

Seductive moves slick and smooth
She gently melted in my hands
A soft massage designed to soothe
Aroused her warm erotic glands

Off on a slow walk through the park
The air was cool, the night was dark
Holding more than hands felt good
Feeling everything we could

Pausing to lie on the lithe ground
Naked alone, no one came near
All we heard was a passionate sound
What a beautiful sound to hear

Our peace disturbed by the breaking dawn
The sky was light pink and blue
There we lay on the soft green lawn
Glistening with morning dew

We went to my place and shared a bath
I said she was welcome to stay
I'd hoped to travel a common path
But she went her separate way

Fantasy Lovers

I'd like to see your hair
Ruffling in the breeze
I'd love to see your face
Smiling back at me
Touching and kissing your breasts
Giving them a squeeze
And finding myself inside of you
Kneeling on my knees

I've had dreams of sleeping
With you by my side
On a bed of water
Creating a tide
Again in a wild frenzy
Our bodies collide
Then after we've passed our crescendo
Letting it subside

I see not a thing wrong
With making love fun
Or making love with you
Underneath the sun
I will wait for the moment
We can become one
As more than lovers in misty dreams
Where our song is sung

Chapter 5: **Lust**

41: Better Left Unsaid: 05/28/1984

42: Friends and Lovers: 06/02/1984

43: Paradise Enough with You: 11/01/1986

44: Off The Wall Lovers: 11/11/1986

45: Friendship Is Fine, But....: 12/12/1986

46: Whatever We Do Let's Do It All Night Long: 12/24/1986

47: Let's Get Naughty: 01/01/1987

Better Left Unsaid

I'd tell you how I feel
But inside you'd be laughing at me
So I'll go on pretending it's not real
And pretending I didn't hear you laughing

Taking my advice on the phone
Would you have listened if you had known
Every word I said to you was influenced
By my desires and not so common sense?

I understand how you feel
You fear our friendship's death and decay
Now I feel passions I've got to conceal
And another loves me that same lonely way

So she will go on pretending
While locking her heart in a cell
It's a sentence that's never ending
Because we are both too afraid to tell

Maybe sometimes more can be said
By not saying anything at all
But I'm gonna climb you're wall instead
And lady, I don't care how far I fall

You told me to follow my dreams
Now I've decided which ones to pursue
As the rivers are fed by streams
Know that all my dreams flow straight to you

Friends and Lovers

We're closer now than ever we've been
Holding strong two lights that burn
Down the darkest roads and dead ends
We'll walk on without a turn
The best of friends

There are times I see a beauty
Transcending perfect friendships
I dream of you in a nighty
The lace off your shoulder slips
OH so pretty!

I held you sleeping as you were
Lost in thought, you in my arms
Yet it seemed no more than a blur
Seeing myself in my dreams
As your lover

Making love on a straight beam
We could do it, you and me
As long as we both share our dreams
I don't see why we can't be
Friends and lovers

Paradise Enough with You

Back home where it is cold in early November
A warm breeze carries passion whistling throughout the air
Share with me this fantasy we'll both remember
Our bodies as one, the passionate touching of our hair

I'd love to bathe with you in a tropical pool
And shower together under a rushing waterfall
On an island in the sun where love is the rule
And the hustle of New York isn't welcome here at all

I ache to feel your heart beating against my chest
Even on top of the North Pole holding you would be nice
Snuggling to feel the warmth of your naked breasts
To be alone with you is enough paradise

Here I see everything in a different light
I can see the woman you are and the girl you were
My desire soars to you like a meteorite
Crashing here where my love is no longer a blur

Off the Wall Lovers

Take a break for a little seductive fantasy
And imagine making love in total privacy
With a microphone on to amplify every sound
Infatuation can be so passionately profound

Hear every moan and every groan rattling the walls
And on your bare bottom cheeks, the slapping of my balls
Many off the wall lovers would find it erotic
Even your parakeets would think this was exotic

I've been longing for a sexy make-up magician
A whole lotta woman and some sexual submission
This is getting outta hand so let's get into bed
Baby, I wrote this for you because of what you said

I can't help it, when I think of you I can't get enough
My mind starts to wander into all that sexy stuff
I've heard it can be fun when it gets a little rough
And it's my desire to have you in the buff

It's time to wake up, no more dreams, the fantasies must end
My heart is beating for the night when it won't be pretend
And all of the sounds echo back and forth in full motion
Even China will wonder, "What's The Commotion?"

Friendship Is Fine, But...

I think it's time for a sincere confession
Before this becomes a clouded deception
I can no longer be the Joe that you know
Because I want to get something going with you

I'm not the same man; I hope our changes rhyme
It's been a long while, a lot's happened in the mean time
I've met a lot of girls and a lotta woman too
It'd sure be nice to get something going with you

Women are rarely what they put on for show
And I've been with enough phonies to know
None of them can touch you, not even any two
I'd really love to get something going with you

Most guys want it before you'll give it away
Then they expect you to do what they say
You need not give me anything; my love is free
How would you like to get something going with me?

Whatever We Do Let's Do It All Night Long

Let's go for a ride and park in the shadows
We'll keep warm on a cold night and fog up the windows
Kissing and touching and making love in the back seat
Steam rising off our bare bodies from our heads to our feet

Hey sweetness, I wanna love you all undressed
And baby I'm not givin' your body a rest
Sexy lady, be with me and you won't be afraid
'Cause when you're in love,
making love's more fun than getting laid

We'll find an all night nightclub and dance until dawn
I want to be with you till the band's packed up and gone
Whatever we do baby, let's do it all night long
And if we haven't sweat enough we'll dance to this love song

I'd be happy just to wake up in your arms
And for breakfast we can share a bowl of Lucky Charms
Just in case you haven't had enough love for one night
We will keep on going for a little afternoon delight

Let's Get Naughty

I've been searching for a way since the first time we met
To start your juices flowing, to tease your love nest wet
I finally found the fuel to make your love ignite
Ooh Baby, I wanna get naughty with you tonight

When I get next to you my body starts to quiver
And I've got the touch to get you flowing like a river
My heart isn't the only muscle that you excite
Mmm, How would you like to get naughty with me tonight?

So you don't misunderstand anything I've said
I want to go home with you and make love in your bed
I'll leave if there's another guy you want to invite
Or maybe you'd rather get naughty with me tonight

Making love isn't something I want to do alone
And it isn't worth it if we do it on the phone
I have wanted you since I first had you in my sight
You're the only one I wanna get naughty with tonight

Chapter 6: **Seven-Year Obsession**

Lisa, Should I Play Guitar?

It's lonely in my empty room
Maybe I will build a wall
You said I'll be hearing from you soon
Do I dare hope you'll really call?
Lisa, say you will finally call

My love's imprisoned in this heart
And you can set it free for me
More than once it's been torn apart
And so I've thrown away the key
Lisa, will you help me find the key?

In my mind I have grown confused
This is as clear as I can say
My heart is true but has been used
I ask you before it falls away
Lisa, will you love me all the way?

Lisa, do you think I've gone too far?
I have been dreaming of you from afar
Am I worth your time if I play guitar
And sing my songs in a dim smoky bar?
Lisa, should I sing in a broken down bar?

Lisa, what do you want me to do?
Try to start over if I knew where to begin?
Try to forget you with my heart broke into?
Broke in two by feelings hidden within
Lisa, in you, the key is hidden within

Lisa, You Break My Heart

No I won't bother you anymore
Or dream about you down on the floor
Any more than I would a common whore
And you know that isn't under my hat
I have too much on my mind for thoughts like that
But I think I should let you know
Lisa you break my heart

Why do I keep trying to phone?
"Call me later, call me back tomorrow"
The reasons I call I don't want to know
But I fear that I call you all too often
And love never as one cannot fall apart
So here's one last call to let you know
Lisa you break my heart

I must have forgotten that love is naive
It's made me foresee what can never be
And beautiful children only my mind can conceive
For my love will remain forever a fantasy
Because I've grown too thick-headed to believe
A lonely life without love, without you
Is this man's destiny

I know your pain as something we share
I opened my ears and my heart to you
How can you treat me as if you don't care?
I'd have to be a fool to keep calling you
So I hope you're not home the next time I phone
"Call me later, call me back tomorrow"
Woman, you break my heart!

The Night Before

Hey Lisa, how do you get hooked up with lemon men?
Every time we talk it's happening again
And now you're fucking one who is already married
Forgotten his promise till he's dead and buried
Lisa, don't you want a man of your own?

I have experienced the quandary you now feel
A damsel sought undercover love she could steal
Surprised was I to see a couple in the paper today
A photograph captured on her white wedding day
Confidentially with me the night before

Forgive me if this isn't what you want to hear
But to see you married is my deepest fear
If the only way to have you for the rest of my life
Is behind the back of my unknowing wife
I'd deceive a maiden and be married

I Want Into Your Heart

Sitting here alone, all these miles away
All I can think about
is taking off your negligee`
But love can't survive on lust and passion
For they are no more
than a temporary sensation

Your pants can wait, I want into your heart
Love takes its own sweet time
and my heart has had a head start
I'll never push you into anything
I'm in to making love in love;
I don't want a one-night fling

To feel your heart beating in sync with mine
Can only be accomplished
if we let our love combine
I hope the void isn't too far to cross
Let's go away together
and make up for all we've lost

It's all my fault, this ever growing void
Considering all the days and nights
we could have enjoyed
If I had wings I'd fly my way across
I'd hold on to you till my lips
were covered with your lip-gloss

Two Friends from the Past

I want an adventurous woman
Willing to dare a daring young man
A heart unafraid of primitive play
I am ready and waiting for the day
We're in harmony as a passionate duet
With mutual desires impossible to forget

But that isn't all I want from you
No pretty lady, though it's all true
The desires I feel sprang from my heart
Telling me, for too long we've been apart
I want to share a love that will always last
And I don't want to wind up two friends from the past

What's The Point?

What's the point of attempting to explain?
What's the point of making it clear and plain?
What's the point when my love will not refrain?
What's the point when there's nothing left to gain?
What's the point if I cannot break the chain?
What's the point if I'm not welcome in your domain?
What's the point with so much distance between the twain?
What's the point when there's nothing to obtain?
What's the point in holding back the rain?
What's the point in trying to stop this train?
What's the point if I can't win my heart's campaign?
What's the point if there are no heights to attain?
What's the point in living with this pain?
What's the point when you wash love down the drain?
What's the point when the thought gives me brain strain?
What's the point when nothing's left I may retain?
What's the point when all my words come out profane?
What's the point when friendship's lost in vain?
What's the point in us being friends again?
What's the point in playing a cruel head game?
The point is you're not the one to blame!

Isn't It A Shame?

Lisa, it seems a bit ironic now
Wasn't I the one who wrote the friendship vow?
I vaguely remember, wasn't it forever?
It's a shame we will never wind up together

But as our friendship's falling down
Oddly enough my reflection shows no frown
While on the surface my hide's as tough a leather
Deep down underneath I still wish we'd wind up together

Your Loss...!

Should I feel bad about not feeling bad
For losing the one true friend I have ever had?
I would if I'd not lost it a long time ago
And replaced it with a feeling you'll never know

Nor will I grieve losing my love for you
I cannot miss a love that I never gave to you
All things with beginnings must also have ends
I will not feel bad if we are no longer friends

Don't change your mind and hope that I persist
I cannot resurrect what never did exist
You won't catch me crying because this is your loss
You never gave my love a chance to get across

Chapter 7: **The Point**

Friends We Must Be

There'll always be a part of me that wonders
Yet between my ears your reply still thunders
I write on this dead tree
Must friends we always be?

My heart pumps confusion deep within my brain
Cleansing my mind of all sanity and pain
Voices kept asking me
Must friends we only be?

Friendships hardly deserve the label "ONLY"
In my twisted confusion I've grown lonely
But now clearly I see
Friends we must always be!

Just because I'll always be in love with you
Cannot be considered reason enough to
Go our separate ways
We must be friends always!

A Possibility

Possibility
Our future forms unseen
Maybe we can be
The friends we should have been

Or futility
Which echoes from before
That which you gave me
I wanted so much more

Before gravity
Brought back reality
Friendship was confused
When fancy over snoozed

Past calamity
Brings fertile soil new life
Making you my wife
A possibility

There I go again
You see I can't pretend
Even as your friend
I'll feel it till the end

Hold On Lisa Hold On Till Then

Lisa, do you know how bad I feel
For the truth I told became unreal?
I had to tell you
No matter what the cost
Friendship wasn't all I'd lost
My honor and my pride
Ran off in shame to hide
Because I lied to you
ALL ALONG, All Along, all along

Lisa, what if we began again?
Do you feel that you could be my friend?
After all my lies
Would you still believe me?
How close would you allow me?
Please don't let it die away
We'll find another way
To become friends again
So hold on till then, hold on till then

Lisa, why should you trust me this time
When even this song can't trust it's own rhyme?
Battling within me
That's just the way I am
Embracing the words I damn
Am I a hypocrite
For faults that I admit?
Guess I'm not so perfect
Guess I'm still in love, still in love with you

Every Night

Coming home on a cold Autumn night
Tired from another rough night at work
A beer, some tunes and I'll be alright
Until I go back to playing store clerk
I'm alone now, there's no one in sight
Then I picture you and get a sly smirk
A song comes on, two lovers combine

Thinking of you makes me wish you were here
Sometimes I pretend that you are mine
Which goes to show you the power of beer
Sometimes I pretend everything's fine
Hopelessly hoping to hide from my fear
Past the shade comes a shimmering light
Unable to sleep I try to doze off

A fantasy, two lovers unite
Enjoying a slow and passionate boff
The fantasy, a dream takes to flight
Your figure beneath me holds me aloft
AWAKE!
A whiff of reality returns
And I'm yanked to the ground out of your arms

Every Night *(continued)*

The emptiness within my heart burns
Incurable by Tums or Lucky Charms
My heart accepts only what it earns
And awaits yours with wide open arms
The dream is over, I still can't sleep
This fantasy land should be swept away
I must avoid getting in too deep

Every craving may become my minds prey
The mountain I climb might be too steep
The thought alone could be more than I weigh
Is it wrong to think of loving you?
But that's all it is, an innocent thought
Ignoring love from your point of view
While hoping to catch the love that I sought

A desire, two friends together
Yearning slowly turning up side down
The feeling, falling, a lost feather
This heart beneath a mountain of down
CRUSHED!
In my hands love resembles bamboo
Despite all I've learned, no lesson was taught

NO ON

I've tried to turn you on
And now I'll give it one more go
But time and time again
Your answer still is NO
I'd like to change
The situation all around
I wanna turn your answer
Upside-Down

Blinded by love
And I can't tell which end is up
A parrot gave me a love potion
To pour in your cup
But that would be unfair
It wouldn't be true love
Instead I'll listen to
The un-caged morning dove

I've pondered this equation
For so long I'm turning gray
But that's OK
So long as I don't have to pay
A solution exists
To help love come of age
A flip of the switch
A turn of the page

Chapter 8: **Veiled In Shadow**

Take Away My Blue

There's no way to change your mind no matter what I do
Even if I lose every inch of my fat
I know I'll never meet another woman like you
That can make my heart pound, make it beat like that

I don't understand how you can turn my love away
C'mon Lisa don't walk away from me
Love feels so fine I don't want to wait another day
I want your heart from now until eternity

I want you Lisa, I wanna have some fun
I wanna love you `cos you're the only one
I'd shower you with gifts and then shower you with me
We'd be gettin' clean while we were gettin' dirty

What will you say if I pretend to be another me?
I wish there was someone I could turn into
But none of that would matter if you'd come out and play
'Cos you could change my life, take away my blue

NY City

"Come to the city, your poetry has style
If you don't move to New York I'll...."
What will you do? What will you do? !
I'd really like to know
I might pack up and go
Though I'm not sure what I'd be getting myself into
Nothing could hold me back if I was getting into you

If your emotions reflected mine
Instead of leaving them behind
I'd find a way to get away
But I don't own a car
And things the way they are
I'd be no closer to my desired destiny
Than I'd be if I remained here in Schenectady

Surely you must know by now what dreams I see
I remember what you told me
"Follow your dreams!" Follow my dreams?
You've said it before
So I'll tell you again
Whether I'm awake or asleep, it doesn't matter when
I want to love you with more than just paper and a pen

Money doesn't add up in my head
Nothing adds up except the words you've said
They add up and down, they add all around
Is my formula wrong?
Why's it taking so long?
There must be a silent way to destroy the dollar sign
The only thing I really want is to make you mine

Veiled Beauty

If I ask you where you are going
If I remind you where you've been
Would you deny what's exposed and showing?
Would you protest that I am cold and mean?

The next time I call you nothing will be new
`Cos you'll never show what's inside your heart
Cover up the love repressed inside of you
You're a pretty painting, not a work of art

From the direction your life has been going
Nothing surprises me that I've seen
Hide away what you don't want them knowing
Spray paint over an artistic scene

Pretending you know where you're are going
Avoiding the Hell where you've been
Realize there is no perfection
To be found within the perfect scene

Shadows

I got up the nerve to give you one more call
The answer I got wasn't worth the fall
You gave up so maybe I should give up too
I'm itching to move on, or is that just fungus in my shoe?

I wasn't good enough to be your lover
Or was I too good? You make me wonder
I've made more a shambles of your life than mine
I should never have tried to cross the line

Now that I have drawn a new line to cross
I must step over the fear of love loss
The only thing standing between love and me
Are the shadows through which I cannot see

What Are We Waiting For?

Your song lilts like a whistling parakeet
Touch the paper and feel the rhythm on this sheet
Of all the songs I've penned there is no finer tune
You're the song I want to sing, mine are picayune

If you think you're out of key you couldn't be more wrong
Lyrics intertwined with chords, you're no common song
Word after word I write, but me, I'm out of key
The gate stays locked till you're in harmony with me

I'll search through every note that I have not explored
Sooner or later I'll discover your lost chord
Some songs come naturally, some must be lived through
Only time will tell if I can tune up with you

The words are all there, but the songs are incomplete
I can't play them for you, my songs are all effete
Yet if we were together you could feel the beat
Of this song you've inspired in one who is aesthete

Truths That I Refuse To See

Lately all I see is what enters through my eyes
If I saw deep inside my heart I'd be in for a surprise
But I deny new love in hopes of touching yours
When I could have it all now if I opened up the doors

Trapped within my own heart and lost inside my mind
But I fear not what I may lose I fear what I will find
The emptiness goes on into infinity
And yet my mind is filled with truths that I refuse to see

I could have the love that requires a closed door
But I'd rather have the kind that brings so much more
Silently love waits for me I need only ask
But your love's the love I want and It's not within my grasp

From in my crystal ball your light shines through the dun
Though a million may surround me my eyes see only one
I'll always wish that I could change reality
If I wasn't so serious I'd be a comedy

I'd do anything for you anything at all
I'd walk one hundred eighty miles to make a local call
But the phone's back on you're eleven tones away
The next best thing's not good enough not good enough at all

Chapter 9: **The Dream Is Over**

67: In the Night Sky: 07/01/1988

68: The Unveiling: 09/27/1988

69: Deja Vu - Happening All Over Again: 01/01/1989

70: You're Where I Wanna Be: 02/14/1989

71: Under Waterfalls: 07/17/1989

72: Finally Through: 11/01/1989

73: On The Outside: 06/07/1992

In the Night Sky

Take me to the places you like to be
Show me the sights that only you can see
Open your heart and read me your thoughts
Release them for me like a swarm of juggernauts

Further than the places I've been
Beyond horizons yet unseen
Rise the answers to my deepest dreams
Where my passions escalate and exceed the extremes

A vision, this woman within my grasp
Seems more like a dream from a forgotten past
I wake up feeling good but will the feeling last?
What am I to do in a reality so vast?

I've soared through the night sky to cast a rainbow
The storm's off in the distance caught in the wind flow
No thunder can shake the love from my heart
No lightning can keep us apart
No wonder you have inspired my art

The Unveiling

Wide eyed men may look at you
And know that you are beautiful
Yet they are blind
For they see only with their eyes
They see beauty only where it lies

Vision can't reveal love to me
For I let my heart lead the way
And I can see
Deeper than two hundred miles away
And hear it in every word you say

The world seems so dark sometimes
But you cast my shadows away
Open your eyes
And see that I can open your heart
Beyond the painting hides a work of art

Fools would put you on display
Or keep you safely tucked away
But no, not I
In my heart neither one may be applied
Open yours up and let my love inside

Deja Vu - Happening All Over Again

The number you have reached
254-8433
Has been DISCONNECTED
No further information is available on
254-8433
Again I have left my heart unprotected

No hurricanes will hit Florida today
`Cos they're all spinning in my gray
No alligators will eat you
`Cos they're all feasting inside me
No tidal waves will sweep you away
`Cos someone else has already swept you away
No treasures will cause my heart to melt
`Cos the gold within my heart can't be touched, only felt
No fuel was enough to make your fire burn
And Fools Gold is worthless; when will I learn?

You're Where I Wanna Be

I've had a lot of time to think
My thoughts have found a place to sink
My very own words have forced me to question
If my love for you is instead an obsession

Well, so what if I'm obsessed?
That just makes me more fun undressed
Even in the real world, when I'm wearing clothes
There's no concealing it, my desire still shows

You've told me more than once to move
I would move anywhere for you
You say I'd hit the big time in the city
I'd only go to find comfort in your kitty

You wonder why my heart still longs
When love's bound within words and songs
But I don't mind `cause it feels the same to me
No matter where you are, you're where I wanna be

Under Waterfalls

Under waterfalls
I'd rather be swimming in your pool
Cooling off in your lagoon
Even paradise is a desert without you

Your smile shines on me
As it sets between your pyramids
What a view between the two
Even a desert is paradise within you

The Sun shines on me
As it sets between the coconut trees
The view is very pretty
But it's nothing compared to the view between your....

Burning sensations
Bring pleasure with every shining ray
The pain is driven away
When two unite and come to a conclusion

Finally Through

I feel new hope rising inside me
There's a soft light, at last I can see
It's time to plot a new course on my old map
I realize I'm finally free of this trap

I knew who you were, now I know who you're not
You're not the kind of woman I want
I want to see real love inside of real eyes
One thing's for sure, that's not love between your thighs

If you could feel like me you'd be feeling fine
Sex isn't love and you'll never cross the line
Instead you cut it and snort it up your nose
Your love's always on it's way, but when it comes it goes

I wouldn't give up but now I don't have to try
There's no more pain, I don't have to cry
You're free of my dreams, I no longer need you
As friends or as lovers we're finally through

On the Outside

Another fast train took you for a ride
Made your heart beat faster every time he lied
He really had his shit together
On the outside

Why trust men with a world of lies to hide?
My soul has shivered every time you've cried
But still you've always left me
On the outside

Baubles are pretty but merely tricks to be tried
They are traps set for you to fall inside
Superficial glitter only makes you pretty
On the outside

A man can't give you what he hasn't got inside
And you can't quench your thirst from an empty cup
At least I'm only messed up
On the outside

I've never hidden how I feel inside
And waited a long time with my arms open wide
Allow me to express my passion and my love
On the outside

I think it's high time for you and I to collide
Our common ground is shared at the bottom of our slides
Take me in both your hands and take me
On the inside

Chapter 10: **The Recurring Curse**

Hypnocize Me

Run me ragged
Run me down
Run my big fat butt off
Until I drop to the ground

Make me tired
Make me sweat
Make me make a wish
Not to eat what I'll regret

Exercise me
Make it hurt
Then when it's over
Hypnocize my pain away

Booty Camp

I have met the most perfect lady
My eyes are in shock and my heart is on hold
Though to her my thoughts are better left untold
Cause I don't think she'll go for my rolled middle fold

It's too bad because I'd do anything
To be the man she'd love and the one she'd hold
The fire in my eyes burns off this old blindfold
And the one burning in my heart makes ashes of the cold.

Her personality is just right
Her face is the fairest since the time of Snow White
Everything about her is everything I like
My Lord she's got a body that is way outta sight!

She smiled at me and I fell for her
I nearly peed my pants right there on the spot
She has inner fire that makes my muscles hot
While we push up and down I get what I don't get a lot

Her energy makes my heart beat fast
The girl of my dreams is awake with me at last
I was overwhelmed sweating with this pretty lass
I think it's time I lost a few pounds off my ass!

Loving You

Years searching through endless haystacks

getting pricked by needle after needle,

wondering how they could be so easy to find

and so hard to hold on to

One day, finding the sharpest needle of all,

but one fashioned from the softest gold

which cannot puncture even hands as soft as mine.

To hold something so pure in my hands

when we have hugged,

even for a few seconds,

filled me with absolute happiness

Hidden From Me

In my mind, climbing the highest mountain

looking around at the wondrous sights

feeling as if I have achieved the greatest of heights

for a moment, feeling complete

Swirling clouds drift away

revealing a higher mountain unseen before

one that reaches into the heavens

so high the peak remains obscured

I want to go there

I want to see what it looks like

I want to know what has remained hidden from me

I want to feel what I have never felt before

Crossroads

I don't know what the point of love is
It seems like an endless road of empty gas stations
on a hill that goes down forever
I can't turn around because
there's no gas left in the pumps to go back up the hill
and as long as I keep going down
There is somewhere to go
Otherwise I may as well pull over for good
It's too far to walk back and
I've already been where the road came from
so what's the point?
If only someone else was traveling the same road
I could hitch a ride and the loneliness would end

So here I am, at a crossroads in my life
at the same time you are at one in yours
I only wish that our roads were crossing a path
that went in the same direction

Unrequited Love

I've been in love so many times
I've lost each one to passion crimes
With all of my heart, to the core of my soul
I love you and now I feel free to let you know
The barrier of marriage has fallen to the ground
Now friendship's all that's left to seek a way around

The question is so hard to ask
Once more my friendship is a mask
Concealing from you my inner most hope
While friendship is strung up on the end of a rope
Am I betraying your trust by following my heart?
Are my feelings something I should never impart?

If I hide this, is it a lie?
Will my love for you live or die?
Is it better to leave, to run away
Without letting you know my heart wants me to stay?
A lifetime of dreams keep telling me I must go
But I can't walk away without letting you know

So with one breath I'll say goodbye
And with the next I'll start to cry
For when I tell you what my heart feels
Our friendship will suffer for all it reveals
But this is my fate, to never have love returned
I am unworthy of yours, a love I have not earned

Emptiness Within

A dream I dreamed about you
About you falling in love with me
We were watching the night sky
Laying on a blanket
On the fifty yard line
Of our high school football field
I kept hoping your heart could fall for me
Like stars to gravity
I wished on one and my wish came true
As you turned to look in my eyes
Our arms reached around each other
Holding on for our lives
We kissed for the first time
And it felt so real
So unbelievably real
My heart was filled with a happiness
I've only dreamed that I could feel
It overwhelmed me so
That I was pulled out of my sleep
And for a moment I could feel
Your hands, your lips still there
Only to feel the emptiness in my arms
Racing straight into my heart
I cried out an echo with my tears,
"God, why is it always a dream?
It's always just a dream"

Chapter 11: **After the Fall**

81: A Lover's Serenade: 06/05/2001

82: The Fall: 10/27/2001

83: Desire No More: 10/27/2001

84: Feminine Fire: 10/31/2001

85: Vegetarian Spam: 11/09/2001

86: Valentine's Day Piercing: 02/08/2002

A Lover's Serenade

My fingers touch the dormant strings
Making silent vibrations quiver with sound
My orb opens up unfurling its wings
Lifting my soul high off the trembling ground

My heart pounds with an endless beat
Reflecting the trembling within my hands
The song is played until it's complete
Which leads to new beginnings in exotic lands

On paper, as a scenic esplanade
My feelings transformed into verse that I write
But on this guitar with a serenade
Love is in the air when my poetry takes flight

The Fall

An autumn evening walk

Hearing the crinkling beneath my feet

Of the fallen leaves shattering

Fallen like my heart in defeat

Desire No More

No More Desire
Anywhere inside of me
I've lost the will to love
And the will to live
Has been thrown to the wolves
Like a bone with blood
Freshly dripping from the meat
Flowing slowly towards
The mouth of a hungry wolf
And when it's jaw crushes
The hollow white shell
To expose the prize within
The ravenous animal tears in
And devours all traces of me

Feminine Fire

Another love died

Before it was born

I opened my heart

With hope and desire

I should not have broken

The promise I'd sworn

To protect my heart

From feminine fire

Vegetarian Spam

You send me forwards in e-mail
Forwards begging me to fail
For I won't send them to my friends
They'll meet only with recycled ends

Making wishes is a waste of time
Even ten seconds would be a crime
But since I know it won't come true
Is it a crime to wish what I wished with you?

So next time you decide to send wishes my way
Consider what I wish for each and every day
Don't bother forwarding anymore to me
I know they don't come true, 'cos you're not here with me

Valentine's Day Piercing

I wish I could say
That it is just an ordinary day
So I wouldn't have to hurt
So I wouldn't have to feel this way

I wish I could die
Or forget how to feel and how to cry
Cupid's pierced my heart again
Forced me to fall for another friend

I don't want to know
How golden and fun your new currents flow
I don't want to meet the lucky one
Who has stolen my wishes and won

Won your heart instead
He makes me wish I'm already dead
But all my wishes were swept away
My pierced heart bleeds this Valentine's Day

Chapter 12: **Knight Fall**

87: A Shadow by The Lake: 08/06/2002

88: Halloween Knight: 10/12/2002

89: Seasons Fall: 10/31/2002

90: Does She Think Of Me?: 10/14/2003

91: I Saw Your Smile Today: 10/14/2003

92: Losing Perspective: 07/07/2007

A Shadow By The Lake

It's that day again, that forever afternoon
I'd forgotten all about it like two years ago
But yesterday someone reminded me too soon
And I think the book store is a better place to go

No one will notice if I'm in my spot or not
I'm sure you won't go to see if I show my face
And with my luck, just like the love I never got
I'm sure someone else will be there to take my place

There's no reason to go, not even old times sake
Tuesday night will never be a walk in the park
If only I could find a shadow by the lake
If not for all the lights I could hide in the dark

My heart knows all too well the sparks that made it blind
Of loves never fostered and friendships that erode
Reflections from the lake will invade my lost mind
With every burst of rockets glare my heart will explode

Halloween Knight

This Halloween I fear the coming of your light
By day I am filled with a darkness black as night
His shadow clouds my eyes to see your face no more
For I'll never be your Knight in shining armor

When all the Saints arrived my demons lurked within
With their number marching, did Valentine sneak in?
Is he a myth like the archer angel Cupid?
Tempting Amour, how could I have been so stupid?

For this Queen, the battle was never mine to fight
Like the Quasi fool, I'm dubbed All Hallows Eve Knight
Seeking sweetness behind each good door where I knock
Only to be handed grief as hard as a rock

You celebrate the anniversary of life
While a wish is made to bring me a deadly knife
Carving the pumpkin and removing all its seeds
Unlike Jack's hollowed head, my empty heart still bleeds

Seasons Fall

Each night underneath the moon
Imagining your hand holding mine
Every sublime summer afternoon
Walking together in the sunshine

I want to see the color of your skies
After a breeze makes the clouds depart
Skies I see in your wide blue open eyes
Reflected back from within your heart

The flame within the orange orb
This candle waits for the birthday cake
Burning brighter than fireworks in the Park
On Tuesdays hot summer night by the lake

The hollow headed monster rides once more
Headless maybe, but not nearly a heartless soul
The Halloween Knight torched the sleeping lore
To write of love buried deep in his fiery hole

Each innocent thought I think of you
Betrays me and I want your raw desire
Every time you speak I see your lips
And taste my lonely heart's raging fire

I've been looking back into the past
To find the love hidden forever after
Been listening for whispers at speeds too fast
To hear you cry the sound of passions laughter

Seasons Fall (continued)

Every cold, rainy morning
I want to hold you and entwine
This Ogre's dream you are adorning
Wrapped tightly together, we combine

I can't write words with passion enough
To express feelings moving within my heart
Surging with softness pretending to be tough
All the while knowing it's time for us to part

Standing beneath a hot shower this morn
Loosening muscles stiff from stillness and cold
With no one to share warmth this life is forlorn
Hard porcelin walls grown over with mold

Seasons fell while I slept last night
I awoke to snow layered on the dying red leaves
The first fall in Fall made the colors turn white
Cold air surrounds me unlike the blanket snow weaves

In a winter night's snowfall
The snow reflects the ambient light
Listen, You can hear them fall
The beats of my heart, in the quiet night

While walking to work it fell
With crunching beneath each step that I took
A cutting north wind felt colder than Hell
Lost in the snow squal where no one will look

Does She Think of Me?

I wonder does she think of me,

Does she ever ask herself what became of me?

Is there never a time when I cross her mind?

When I've put forth my heart with love so totally blind

I cannot shake her face from in front of all before my eyes

I'd sell my soul to replace the dire truth with the clarity of lies

Does she recall when I was less a fool pretending to be a friend

While my heart lied to hide the feelings it constantly bled?

Now I am alone, more alone than I had ever known

anyone could ever be, could ever feel completely un-free

I'm sitting here in silence wondering, does she think of me?

I Saw Your Smile Today

Today I saw your figure through the glass

I saw your eyes when you turned to see who was there

I saw your smile and could not keep mine from peaking

From behind the frown I have worn since the last time I saw

Your figure, your eyes, your smile.

Through the glass, I saw you today

Losing Perspective

Can you sense my lament raining for turning my back on you?
Can a voice travel twenty-five thousand miles and still be heard?
My eyes be damned yet still I see your face through the waterfall
Giving me hope you can hear me behind our imaginary wall

The world spins in twenty-four hours, carrying a new day in tow
Yet eternity stands in the way of reversing half a turn or letting it go
Full circle to meet your eyes lifting from the sorrow of dismay
As the light of morning burns away the mourning of yesterday

Awaken to grasp twenty-five hundred days have made the miles fade
But not the memory of the pain freshly exposing the fool that I made
Living in a past rushing ahead more rapidly than unclean feet can run
Toward a destination as empty as the one I can't stop running from

Chapter 13: **Maggie-Margret & Heather**

93: Life Long Wife: 02/04/1982

94: Butterflies: 08/11/1982

95: Maggie Maybe: 10/10/1982

96: Warm Hands and Wet Feet: 12/26/1982

97: Staying Home - New Year's Eve: 12/31/1982

98: In the Drifts: 01/31/1983

99: Fool In The Rain: 06/22/1983

100: Your Great Charade: 09/04/1983

101: Deja Vu - Haven't I Been Here Before?: 08/11/1984

Life Long Wife

Well I've lived such a lonely life
So I'm looking for a life long wife
One that will love me and never shove me
Yeah I'm searching for a life long wife

Well I've slept through a dreamless life
Had fantasies of making my wife
I want a family, not just a fantasy
Yeah I want to make love to my wife

I wanna have a peaceful life
So I'm looking for a life long wife
To raise our children and be my woman
That's who I want in a life long wife

Butterflies

It was five years ago this week
When I gazed into two beautiful eyes
She was a girl, not yet at her peak
And I was a boy filled with butterflies

And now so much time has passed
As I glance back into those eyes
She went from a girl to a woman so fast
But I'm still a boy filled with butterflies

She gave birth to a daughter
Much to my surprise
In my heart I'll always want her
And to see those beautiful eyes

Searching beyond my reflection
Through her eyes to her soul
Looking for a small section
She will let my heart control

I wonder every time I kiss her
Does she realize
I want to tell her that I love her
But I'm still a boy filled with butterflies

Someday I hope she'll discover
The words I write are not lies
And I wish that I could forever
Gaze into those beautiful eyes

Maggie Maybe

Dear Maggie, Dear Margret, My dear
When I was much younger
My mind filled with great wonder
Each time that I looked in your eyes
But I was afraid you might turn me away
In a direction I'd been turned before

Dear Maggie, My Margret, My dear
As the years passed me by
Tears misted in my eyes
When I heard you loved another guy
And now you've broken up
Time has brushed me with luck
But is it good or bad luck that I've won?

My Maggie, My Margret, My dear
I really hope all my love
Will give you the shove
That you need to fall in love with me
But if you want more time
Before you'll be mine
Then take as much as you need to be free

Warm Hands And Wet Feet

My love for you is plain to see
But I haven't felt yours yet
And when at last I hold your key
I'll pass through your parapet

Though you do not yet realize
The passion I feel now
It doesn't really matter babe
I love you anyhow

I want to live my life with you
And be a family
I'd love to touch you in the nude
And feel you holding me

Let my fingers perform
You've got all the right grooves
I will keep my hands warm
And we will see if I improve

I can learn every step
Teach me all of your moves
Then while I'm getting my feet wet
I'll be wearing loves shoes

While you may never want to share
The feelings that I do
If you ever feel like love
Remember who loves you

Staying Home - New Year's Eve

Tonight I recall last New Year's
Out with close friends but so alone
Spent the eve hiding my tears
But not tonight I'm staying home

It seems like just yesterday
Drowning in a bar with my friends
Talking without words to say
Rambling till the evening ends

I remember their faces
Guzzling small bottles of whine
And vodka with beer chasers
I guess they were all feeling fine

I wonder are you having fun?
Once again you've left me behind
I wonder are you with someone?
My tears are not what makes me blind

As the new year rolls around
I'm by myself, here all alone
I won't let it bring me down
Because tonight I'm staying home

In the Drifts

I can't remember when
So long ago seems like yesterday
In the dead of December
When blind love was mislead astray?

Too soon January came
Winter's wind chill cut like icy knives
I ponder, am I to blame?
For without her I'm un-alive

She's not here to keep me warm
And I'm still wondering why
I need shelter from her storm
Yet I sit still as snow drifts by

No longer can I see clear
Ice seals over both of my eyes
My drums are still, no longer to hear
And I still sit where sun sets die

The air's too cold to survive
Suddenly I have learned to fly
All feeling's gone, am I alive?
While my body lays my soul drifts by

Fool In the Rain

So now I feel like a fool in the rain
Afraid to move on and try love again
Within my heart is one more regret
In spite of the rain love's shoes never got wet

I fooled myself into believing my scam
Pretending to be more than I am
Now as reality surfaces
The mirror exposes my two faces

I feared what the future had in for me
I fought against it and tried to be free
Trying too hard to achieve sublime love
But the passion we shared wasn't enough

My fate's been decided somewhere up there
I'll die with the love I wanted to share
My destiny and I are merging
Preventing our hearts from ever converging

Your Great Charade

And so I suffered from a pain
That stemmed from deep within my brain
Not only for the love that was lost
But also for the friendship deceit cost

And I may never understand
How love and hate both share command
Of feelings that I thought had died
When you told me truths about which you lied

Too high a price for love was paid
When you performed your great charade
With eyes wide open I was blind
My back was turned as you slithered behind

And now at last the truth is out
Your conscience cries consumed in doubt
Could you hear your promises fade
Each time you lied in the bed that you made?

Deja Vu - Haven't I Been Here Before?

Haven't I been here before?
Here at your gate once more
I have opened up this door before
If I do it again
Must I endure the pain
I last felt in the wind and pounding rain?

Woman you blew me away
Like a storm out at sea
Each night I Prayed for the break of day
I thought your blood was warm
Your passion sincere
But no, the heat of the moment I fear

Now with all of my past fears
In spite of my spent tears
My pulse races like it did once before
I would not hesitate
To open your gate
I want to look into your eyes once more

Chapter 14: **Empty Nest**

What Lies Beneath

I once wallowed in self-pity
Froze beneath that witches titty
Now the fire is burning ever more
For this girl who's shown me an open door

A different class of lady
Is what I've found, one less shady
She's revealed an abundance of love
And lusts deception she's risen above

Her aura glitters with beauty
And I feel it surrounding me
Soon she'll be a woman full of love
And I will be the man that fills her up

Never Fall To Troubles

So now I'm seein' sights that I've never seen
I'm flyin' higher than a kite ever flew
And if you'd really like to know what the reason is
It's because Angel, I love you

This love's not like any other that I've had
Because you've shown how much you really want me
You're so unlike any girl I've ever met
I'm tickled that you're part of "WEE"

If we're always honest and face our problems
Then we can talk them out `cos we are best friends
We'll never fall to troubles that break up other couples
What's in our hearts will help them mend

But the best thing about this new love of mine
Is that I'm sharing every feeling with you
I've got a feeling this one's gonna last forever
And we will die before it's through

So let's live our lives together till the end
And be as happy as we possibly can
We both see the same kind of future ahead
I know you'll love me for who I am

Lovely Lady

My lovely lady is an angel to me
She has shown me trust and honesty
Like I have never seen it before
And it's true, I have never seen it before

I have survived the torment of love betrayed
Fallen to depths that left my heart afraid
Yet she has managed to erase my doubts
And brought to once tear'd eyes the moisture of droughts

She too has endured pain from a broken heart
Seduced by lust from a poison dart
First thought to have flown from Cupid's bow
But surely it soared from the darkness below

I can't imagine with the love she gives
That a finer girl on this world lives
In spite of the pain she has suffered
She has caressed the passion I have offered

Time healed old wounds and desire flowed into my life
Perhaps one day she will be my wife
But for now she'll remain my girlfriend
And each of love's struggles ahead we will transcend

Cold as Ice

I'm a very poor man
My pockets are empty, look not even a cent
All I have left is my room
And I'm bein' evicted 'cos I can't pay the rent

I just can't pay the price
The air has gone stale and I'm facing banishment
This room is as cold as ice
Hey, does anybody got another room for rent?

The warmth has been shut off
There's ice on the bed springs and it's four months till May
I want a permanent loft
And when I move in I promise I won't ever stray

I'd love a bed that's soft
And a landlord that won't throw me out in the cold
One that will say "Love's enough
Here's the key, this room is free; Love is worth more than gold

I Wish I Wasn't Me

I've always been the good guy
And everyone I meet would like to be my friend
But of all the people in the world
I wish I wasn't me

I would take instead of give
I'd never fall in love again, I'd be one of the users
Never again one of the losers
If I just wasn't me

I could take my life and stop this pain
If I didn't have to face myself, face the inner me
My soul's too strong to defeat
Oh God, please let me be

If I wasn't me
I could ignore her and forget this loss
But I'm not quite strong enough
Love's always been my boss

I Wish I Wasn't Me (continued)

Now I can't take it anymore
I am losing all my sanity
And the acid in my stomach
Is burning out my brain

Silence is all around me now
I wish the peace surrounding me would enter
I'm certain I would feel better
I wish it would flow through me

But nothing more will ever enter
No love, no peace, no one will ever touch me
I'll never let another rogue
Cut what's left of me

How can I ever be your friend?
You told me it was because I am who I am
That you could tell me all these truths
Oh God, I wish I wasn't me!

What I Want, What I Need; Is It Wrong, Is It Greed?

What I want, what I need
Is a bit of a lot of some stability
I'm all out of blood
There's no more to bleed
I would really enjoy getting back to simplicity

What I want, Is it greed?
Is it greed to want love, love in full flower?
I'd plant desire
Then water the seed
And hope the fruit you bare doesn't fall or sour

What I want, is it wrong?
Is it wrong to want you sharing a shower?
I hope you'll love
Sharing passion with me
I seek your guiding light when I'm in my darkest hour

Are you there, anywhere?
Don't shadow me with your blanket, your cover
It won't mean a thing
You only want fun
When we're finished it's over, when you've cum it's all over

Leave me now, fly away
I need to be alone, here all alone
I've used up my words
I've no more to say
My blood has washed away, my thew is skinned to the bone

An Empty Room Have I

I love you quite possibly too much
And I wish it was last night
I reach to feel your loving touch
And I wish it was last night

Why do you turn from my love, my touch?
Is this slight an oversight?
I'm alone and I want you so much
And I wish it was last night

Now I look around this empty room
And I wish it was last night
I am surrounded with shadows and gloom
And I wish it was last night

You aren't here this darkest of days
And I wish it was last night
Mornings colors have turned shades of gray
Cold slips under the rising light

I remember how happy I was
And I wish it was last night
I remember how content I felt
And I wish it was last night

But last night will never be again
Your love has fallen from your heart
Perhaps the beach last night never should have been
The breeze that carried us away now blows us apart

Chapter 15: **The Darkives**

109: D-archives: 04/10/2002
110: I Give Up, I Quit, Just Let Me Go: 04/22/2001
111: Tired Of Life: 04/28/2001
112: One Heart Too Strong To Live: 05/04/2001
113: Rescued Last: 05/21/2001
114: Tonight's the Night: 05/21/2001
115: What's Living Inside Me: 10/29/2001
116: Flicker: 08/19/2001
117: Not For Kings: 06/26/2003
118: I Want To Lie: 06/09/2001
119: Just Friends: 11/28/2001

D-archives

In the darkness where my naughty side thrives

You can hear a thud each time that one arrives

Hiding in the shadows like past forgotten lives

In the dusty corridors of the poet's forbidden archives

Passing through with a weedy heart would be most unwise

For in this hole of pain, the truth wears a disguise

I Give Up, I Quit, Just Let Me Go

It's hard to smile, it's hard to laugh
When the only thing worth laughing at
Is my miserable fucking life
Filled with nothing and drenched with fat

It's hard to see in the darkness
That surrounds me everywhere I go
I close my eyes and embrace death
For love's embrace I'll never know

It's hard to love without a heart
I gave mine away so long ago
Now she is someone else's wife
And I'm no one you'd want to know

It's hard to want without desire
I don't give a damn any more
I'd rather quit this empty life
And pass through Hades open door

It's hard to know what love is
When no one has ever shown me
A soul is lost that can't be sold
A soul not worth taking for free

It's impossible to save
Not even Jesus Christ will save me
From wasting what our Father gave
And accepting my destiny

Tired of Life

I'm so fucking tired I just want to sleep
Tired of living and being alone
I'm so tired of feeling like this hole is too deep
Nothing is worth the rate on this loan

Where are you my love, where are you tonight
I'm shaking with fear that you're not alone
I can't take the pain, I give up the fight
I'm afraid I may die from fear of the unknown

But I'd rather not know, I'd much rather die
Than to find out you're happy and smiling
While looking in the eyes of another guy
Now my eyes are closing from hours of crying

This may very well be my last words to you
Every time I try to see you, excuses are found
I'd rather die not knowing than find out it's true
Please come and visit, I'll still be lonely underground

One Heart Too Strong to Live

Love deals one last crushing blow
Time and time again my heart has given in
Although my mind always seems to know
It never tries to warn the pulsing orb within

After the collapse begins
My heart marches on like a proud warrior
To the battle that it never wins
With all its inner toughness, it feels inferior

While waging a silent war
No one around me can hear my raging heart
Not even she who I feel them for
Knows the strength of feelings that break the core apart

Rescued Last

Love is nothing, an unreal sensation
Lies told to create sinking ships of relation
But they relate only to those who paid for the cruise
Who believed head over heals in the titanic ruse

I have never seen so many fools fall
Didn't they see the scene with the ship standing tall?
Even those who were lucky to hold on for their lives
Drifted off, freezing the heart of the one who survives

I wonder which fate is worse to be dealt
To be rescued but stripped of the passion once felt
Living for years, empty, lonely and wanting to die
Thinking that dying is better than living a lie

Tonight's the Night

I am alone in my quiet life
My heart awaits this haunting knife
In my hand the blade still dry
Longs for the fate I can't deny

I've walked this road in the distant past
I want this time to be the last
This tangled web I can't untie
Trapped within my own sordid lie

There is a weight I cannot lift
My heavy heart's been lost adrift
My soul sinks deeper from the sky
Tonight's the night I want to die

What's Living Inside Me

It isn't fair to expect you to fill my empty life
It isn't fair to want you to love me as my wife
It isn't fair to pretend you're not with another man
It isn't fair to keep hoping that he won't be the one

But I can't stop from feeling that life is never fair
For me it's never been even close
I've never had the chance to share
I want this pain to go away

I don't want to live another day
If I'm to never hear what I want you to say
But I don't want to hear it if you don't feel that way
I'd rather die than live that lie

I'd rather end these retched nights
I want to pull out this plug and shut off these lights
I want to die, I want to end this misery
I can't take anymore of what's living inside me

Flicker

There's no point in writing another rhyme

Or convincing myself of all my empty lies

My life past and present is one big waste of time

I can't see any reason for a thirty ninth reprise

No one really wants to sing that unhappy song

They just want some cake, I can see it in their eyes

The match is struck, now it's time to make a wish

I wish the same wish every year, when will I realize?

That like the candle left burning for too long

The wick turns to ashes and the flame flickers till it dies

Not For Kings

If one could die of loneliness surely I'd be dead by now
Or from a broken heart, there'd be no beating in my chest
So why do happy know-it-alls insist on giving me false hope
That my afflictions could mercifully free me from this hole?
The dream of rising up high beyond the walls surrounding me
Free of my cage, free of the pain, free of the repetitious laugh
Haunting a fragile mind, making nightmares of the cold reality
That no love will ever requite all that my broken orb has shown
Must be a story for human hearts much weaker than my own
Not for kings like Kong who get shot down off high pedestals

With gawkers and picture clickers
standing on his breast
One voice was heard to say,
"T'was beauty, killed the beast"
But it wasn't true, it's not her fault
he fell so far from the clouds
He knew the risks, knew they'd come
to fire rounds to pierce his heart
He held on for dear life, held on to her
in hopes that his undying love
Could fill his empty heart
for his lonely life would never let him go
With that final thought within his brain
he discovered he was right
For all his loneliness followed him
beyond the soil placed on his grave
Down to a place he knew so well
all the days he lived and walked alone
Where there is no beauty for which to fall,
where his heart at last can rest in peace

I Want To Lie

This curse will haunt me while I'm still alive
I live within a dream I can never explore
This feeling inside continues to thrive
In spite of the ache I want you more than before

If only I could turn and step back in time
To swallow my words mutating truth into lies
I'd rather choke pretending camaraderie's fine
And hope you don't catch love hiding behind my eyes

What has been said I can never take back
My heart wishes it so but my head still says no
It hurts to admit all the strength that I lack
But so much worse is the pain from not letting go

Just Friends

There never was a chance for misguided rhymes
To create an illusion that could fool you forever
Trust becomes a victim of passionate crimes
The cost of embracing a fantasy friendship endeavor

Don't be sorry I feel I can't be your friend
To value our amity only makes matters worse
Whether I like it or not you will not stop being my friend
Once again rejection cries out the words of my curse

Deception guides Arnold's quest of unyielding fear
From the first time it is voiced the echo never ends
I'd sooner die of loneliness than ever again hear
Love's purest phrase of pain, "I just want to be friends"

Afterthought

In retrospect, it occurred to me that the darker chapters of this book might lead one to conclude they are the final chapters of my life. Nothing could be further from the truth, unless I happen to die of natural causes or some unforeseen disaster. Suicide has taken some who I cared for most in this world, I will not be one.

As mentioned previously in the Caveat, I have been afforded an opportunity to review my life, to gain insight through survival and to continue my quest for the two things in life I have yet to understand or obtain. At times I feel conflicted, especially when my feelings are at odds with what I know in my mind. I have many times followed my feelings and later found I had made the wrong choice.

Oftentimes writing poetry has clarified what direction to travel. Other times the path I follow inspires the words and forces changes I'd been resisting inside me. I am reminded of how pride was firmly entrenched in my heart as a catalyst of inspiration until a conversation with my brother caused me to doubt my belief. Eventually that led me to write "3 Seeds" after reading MLK's sermon, "The Drum Major Instinct". Never before had I been so moved and inspired as I felt reading it.

As inspirations come over me, so too will poetry. No matter how beaten down hope has become, somehow it is rejuvenated over and over, filling me with possibilities for the future. Letting go of life would be to give up that hope. Better it is to let go of hate. Change is inevitable and beliefs are only as tangible as unproven thought. I believe as deeply as my heart can beat that I will find love, and faith will find me. I hope the Mayans are wrong, somehow two more years doesn't seem long enough.

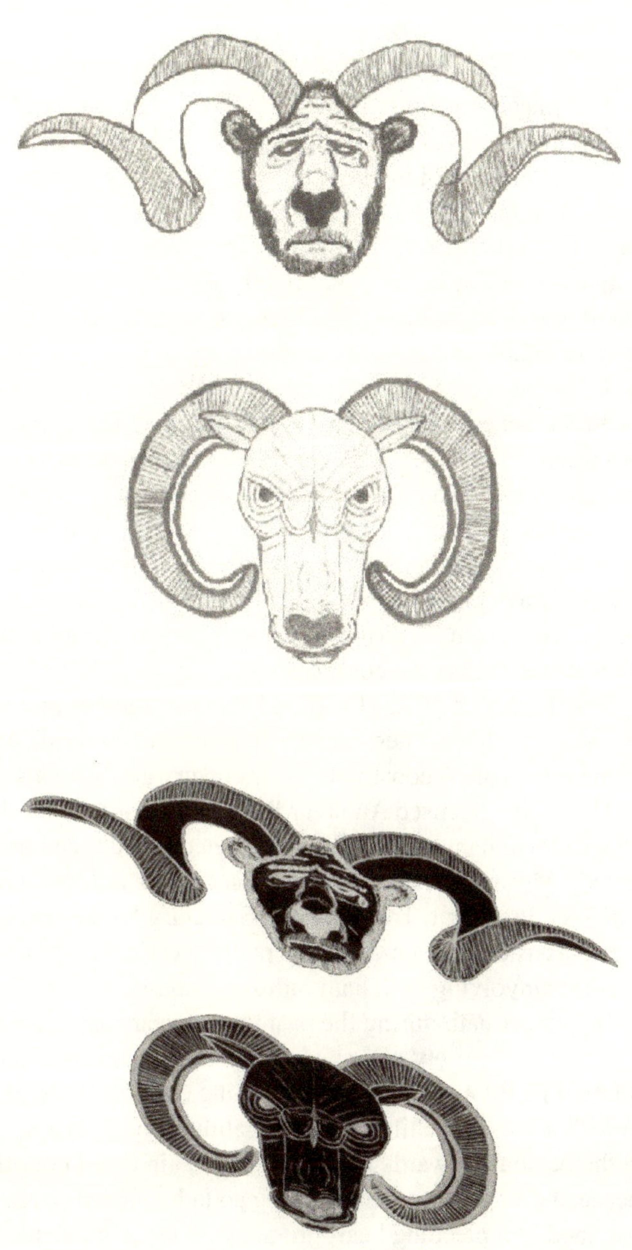

About The Author

JJ Johnson was born in Gloversville, NY in 1963 and later moved with his family to Schenectady in 1979. After graduating from Linton High School in 1981, he attended DeVry Technical Institute in Woodbridge, NJ and Schenectady County Community College from 1981-1984. He spent over four years as a Teacher's Aide with three in English at Schenectady High, formerly Linton. After moving to Richmond, CA in 2006, he returned home to Schenectady in 2007 where he resides through 2014.

JJ has been an active participant in the poetry community and hosted the Schenectady Poetry Horde spoken word open mic for over two years at the Moon & River Café in the Stockade of Schenectady. Passion and Pain is his second collection of poems.

Over the past several years, JJ has been involved as an activist for peace, equality and the environment. Though these issues have always played a part in his life in varying degrees, the trampling of American civil rights, war and Global Warming have made him aware of his own complacency.

In February of 2012 JJ suffered a stroke that left him visually impaired along with weekness on one side and fractal recall. Many of his past memories are reconstructed from poetry and journals entries.

JJ is also a licensed Amateur Radio operator who has been a member of local ham radio clubs and elected board member of the Schenectady Museum Amateur Radio Association, holding the offices of Vice President, Treasurer and Secretary for several terms. He has also assisted with emergency communications and public service events involving both ham radio and non-ham activities.

His career path during the past twelve years has involved helping others in a variety of ways in schools, care, medical and rehabilitation facilities, and in home learning environments. JJ has worked with adults and children with disabilities of all types, reaping the personal rewards where financial gain could not offer inner peace and hopes to continue doing so in his future endeavors. Self described as a bleeding heart progressive and genuine nice guy, JJ believes that freedom of choice is the only way to reach ones spiritual destiny.

Index

Chapter 16: Bonus Poems

120: Un-Stately Swans: 02/15/1995
121: When Everyone Got Paid: 10/12/2011
122: Who's In Control Here!?: 05/31/2011
123: Love Ain't Free: 11/21/2011
124: It's a Dog Eat Cat World - 07/16/2012
125: Opposite Sides of the Sky - 01/27/2012
126: Souls Mate - 07/24/2012
127: Rain Beneath the Rainbow:5/11/2014
128: Rain Drops On My Head:7/12/2014
129: Dark Star: 08/17/2013
130: Unwrapping Your Toys: 12/10/2012
131: Madam Lark of Night: 05/20/2013
132: Scratch Your Mark on My Tree: 07/07/2013
133: Dolphins Song:5/17/2014
134: Blue Horizons Bleed Red Mist: 08/20/2013
135: Dripping Into Death - 07/26/2012
136: After Birth: 09/27/2011
137: Goodbye! - 07/19/2012
138: Goodbye Drips from Your Lips:11/15/2013
139: Rusted Rainbows: 07/06/2013
140: How?: 10/24/2012
141: Jealousy is Such a Bitch: 09/26/2013
142:Masturbating Reminda Me I Am: 10/24/2014
143: Nobody Knows the Trouble I've Sown: 07/04/2013
144: Death-right: 08/05/2013
145: There is Someone Deeper than Dark: 05/04/2012
146: Secret Sins: 11/10/2013
147: Between Reality and Hell: 09/11/2012
148: Hiding Hollow Eyes: 09/09/2011
149: Myst-air-E-girl: 5/13/2014
150: I Remember When: 08/26/2014
151: Nothing Is Real:7/30/2014
152: afraid: 08/18/2014
153: A Hero's Secret: 11/30/2012
154: T-4-2: 10/18/2012
155: The Outline of My Lover: 12/24/2011
156: To One Too Alone - Two Alone, Too Bad: 08/17/2014
157: Mae I Call You Juliet:10/17/2014
158: Nothing Before Me, Nothing Behind: 10/25/2014
159: Ghosts:7/28/2014
160: Passion and Pain: 08/10/2014

{bonus poem 120}

Un-Stately Swans

An eagle eyes an angel on the meaty side of town
Where the the ladies are awaiting to hawk their wares around
I see her strutting at the bus stop every evening
Work was long and oh how I could find comfort in her breathing
My first step down brings her sweet voice as candy to my ears
She asks me each evening but my response she never hears
Now if I was the only one, I'd have said "yes" long ago
I'd take her in and do the sin but my names's not John, I'm Joe

A winter snow with nowhere to go to get out of the cold
The bus slides to a stop, I get off to silence gone unsold
Surely you'll catch your death if you remain out in this storm
I ask if you'd like to sit by the fire, drink something warm
But you say he's watching and expects payment for the time
So I say send him my way to collect mine for his crime
It's his turn to pay for the rape built to enslave his con
Locked shackles bind you to this corner 'til he's dead and gone

Allow your mind to open the next chapter yet un-penned
Let my heart teach yours that beatings pulse is meant to mend
Let my touch bring feeling to the passion lost inside your heart
Let me walk you to a door that opens to a fresh start
Let me open your eyes where the future lies beyond
Let me free your hands of the oppression in those bonds
Let me set your feet free to walk through fields that know no fear
Let my voice say the words no mouth would ever let you hear

Let my feet carry you across the sunrise of a new day
Let me crack the dawn in lieu of spreading crack to lay
Let me show the light you shine is less red, fading into blues
Let me display the way to any path you choose
Let me assure you that he bears redundant blame
Let my arms comfort your soul and push away the shame
Let me lift the weight off your wings to see you carry on
Let the blade of the Knight come to free an un-stately swan

{bonus poem 121}

When Everyone Got Paid

We've got this economy that sucks more than corner whores
Taxes collected don't add up to the garbage on our shores
There's more blow jobs per hour than jobs employers can hand out
If disease was not a problem, I might self-employ and put some out

So why not pay for bridges to get fixed legally on our knees
When the owner of the body is the one who holds the keys?
Health care all for free to make it safe for both rich and poor
No more pimps or madams in control of the revolving door

Politicians would not need to keep secret their dirty secret lives
Well, at least they'd only have to keep them secret from their wives
I am willing to bet there would be so much money to be made
I could lose the bet and still have plenty left to go get laid

Fewer criminals saves the cost to incarcerate so many Johns
While those enslaved for sex would be free to become moms
The end of auctioning bodies to start bidding on E-Bay
When the lady of the evening can finally keep her pay

Where do hookers disappear when they become too old
Is Jesus there that fateful day to save what they have sold?
And who could throw a stone on another fateful day
When Jesus told the sinners to look inside and walk away?

{bonus poem 122;-}

Who's In Control Here!?

I wanna make you watch all my favorite shows
Wanna expose your deepest secret so everybody knows
Wanna watch you cook my dinner from my easy chair
Wanna tell you I don't care if you think life is unfair
Wanna hear water filling up the tub just before my bath
Wanna take all of your money and let you do the math
Wanna smell pancakes and eggs, waking in my bed
Wanna wash the puny brain in your pretty little head
All I wanna do is to control you

I wanna take away your cell phone for my own
Wanna text whenever I am not at home
Wanna sext whenever you're too busy for me
Wanna delete all your contacts, all except for me
Wanna call all your friends and tell `em you can't talk
Wanna listen to your calls and watch you like a hawk
Wanna make your actions echo every word I say
Wanna show you who is boss every single day
All I wanna do is to control you

Who's In Control Here!? (continued;-)

I wanna sit next to you while you steer the wheel
Wanna be chauffeured 'cos that's just how I feel
Wanna let you know when it's time to make a turn
Wanna ride till there's no more gasoline to burn
Wanna tell you when to start and when it's time to stop
Wanna make you evade the law and ignore every cop
Wanna make you drive faster when I'm feelin' slow
Wanna hear you complainin' how I'm always on the go
All I wanna do is to control you

I wanna let you know that you are not alone
Wanna run 'em off the road for talkin' on the phone
Wanna shout that the air and road belong to me
Wanna collect a toll 'cos my road isn't free
Wanna let everyone learn to get out of my way
Wanna end all freedom, it's the price they gotta pay
Wanna give them equal opportunity to fall
Wanna let each one know who is in charge of it all
All I wanna do is control you too

{bonus poem 123;-}

Love Ain't Free

I wanna give you lovin and never get a job
You'll be the only one that can twist my old door-knob
I'll do anything this job requires even on one knee
Cos I always wanna feel like I just won the lottery

I'm a hungry wolf in this dog eat cat economy
I'll always make you happy so long as you keep me
With benefits to keep me a loyal employee
And keep the kitchen cookin' cos' you know that love ain't free

If the way to a man's heart is to fill his empty tummy
Then food will not satisfy my desire for all that's yummy
I'll thank you on Thanksgiving Day for all you give to me
Then gobble-gobble-gobble you up like a bag of Halloween candy

Let go of the hope for a midnight sale coming Black Friday
Cos my never ending comfort is the price you gotta pay
A zillion bucks wouldn't be enough for the loan of my body
Just consider it a bargain to be with someone this sexy

{bonus poem 124;-}

It's a Dog Eat cat World

Snif
Sniff Sniff
Sniff Sniff Sniff
Kitty?
RAWR!
rraaaaa
rraaaa
rraaa
rraa
rra
rr
r
crunch!
Aahhhhhhh
meyummm
meyummm meyummm
meyummm meyummm meyummm

Sniff
Sniff Sniff
Sniff Sniff Siff

{bonus poem 125}

Opposite Sides of the Sky

our skies contrast as night and day
our lives apart as dawn to dusk
if only the years were not so heavy on my shoulders
and so many on my back
break this ancient heart if it were to express its true desire
our hearts harmonize beating no delay
the sound of thunder explodes from my chest
with each word that you express
I feel so close when close my eyes
it burns my soul to dream of you
to kiss the smile you offer me
when deep your eyes invite my gaze
to embrace smooth curves when breasts meet chest
to give you the caress to make a kitten purr
to open you with a lions roar
and devour the sound of your meow
to want too much from too far away in far too many ways
I will never realize these feelings
no matter every one is true
you may as well be on Venus while I am lost on Mars
to love and lose your touch
my heart would surely cease to beat

{bonus poem 126}

Souls Mate

My own heart defies my mind
To explain its expressions
To make sense of this sensation
That pulses through my veins
A flood that uncontained would wash away all thought
To leave nothing but the feeling to impart upon one other
To speak the word of L before the fallout fell
So what's the rush, yet what a rush?!
To be consumed in so hot a fire of desire
That passion merely stokes the embers ever higher
Each word of restless verse
Draws fuel from the souls
That meet their mate when falling sells control
of two hearts to one another
I am yours and you are mine but we own nothing on our own
This bliss, this want to touch our ghosts almost frightens me
It might if not for the sincerety of the words
Forged within the creative kiln of our poetry
To you and to me we'll paint the skies with ecstacy
And on the dawn after the first night
Two hearts glow with a single soothing light

{bonus poem 127}

Rain Beneath the Rainbow

Peering out from behind your dark curtain
The spectacle of your eyes sparkle like white diamonds
That cut through the cloak of sadness wrapped around my heart
Penetrating the shadows that fall away from my desires
Following the line of your long dark hair down across your neck
The slope of your curves lifts my eyes
as your hair flows over your breasts
Washing you from head to toes
while the water washes down over your curves
Like a thunderstorm in the heat o a summers night
Trickling across your flesh like a thousand fingertips
Carrying away the scent of the day
while your skin glistens with moonlight daggers
As the shaddow of my hands moves gracefully across your hills
Dance with my hands and swivel within my touch
As my fingers explore the soft cover
that keeps warm your sensual nest
My deep seeded desire seeks out your berried treasure
Swimming as deeply as the soul can dive
Only your consensual cravings can satisfy my fiery heart
I will not take what does not cry out to be taken in the flood
This river swells beyond the shores that contain it no more
Drowning innocence in a sea of crashing waves
The pounding surf engulfs even the peaks of twin mountains
Skiing down your magnificent snowy slopes
An avalanche of passion cascades across moist flesh
Until the thunder cracks one final time with a bolt of white hot light
And a geyser of lava erupts from beneath the surface of your skin
Nature has a way of leveling obstacles
a single one can never overcome
Until two of one obsession taste each others ancient sins

{bonus poem 128;-}

Rain Drops On My Head

Let me live within your poems
Where your words begin as babbling brooks
That flow after Springs misty rains
Make me breathe in every vowel sound you speak
And exhale consonants across your curves
Your rain washes through my expanding veins
Spray my lips with your rainbow shower
Drizzle chocolate drops of melted coco butter
Swirled in with my Cool Whip cream
Your tornado rages all over me
As your hurricane hurriedly lays waste to my bones
The scent of hot fudge floods my head
Leaving my senses all for dead
Until your lightning strikes my chest
Reawakening my beatless heart
After lightning sparks my heart soon burns
Renewing the pulsing surge of blood
Flooding the halls of my brainless head
I wish to reside on your street of thunder storms
Where cloudbursts pour the heavens dry
Rain down on me from your torrential skies
And gaze upon me with Tararential eyes
Blow me away with the wind of your words
Escaping from your gripping lips
Gasping for air beneath your pounding waves
More Rain, more Rain cum down on me!

Dark Star

Am I the only one who can see you?
You set my sky ablaze with shadows
Cast your phantom over me and allow me to be
Your Black Knight in shining armor
Shoot your dark glow all over me
Illuminate my night with your spray of black-light
Penetrating the flesh with shafts of ultra-violet
Swords, sharper than steel, invisible
Intangible yet cutting into my heart
Filling every thought with embers of desire
From the first look that pierced my mind
Clenching my hands to hang onto your scent
Wishing on Perseid's cast-aways
As they drop to their fiery demise
Imagine with me what you do not believe
Realize with me the laughter of lovers
Keep me looking up at your beauty
Shine with the shimmer of meteors
Don't leave me, don't ever fall from my sky
Keep me wishing even if they never come true
Will them to fruition and let me be with you

{bonus poem 130;-}

Unwrapping Your Toys

When I press your button on the left
You peep with a itsy-bitsy squeak
And then caress the button to the right
Your fluffy bear begins to speak
When I push the button in your belly
You up and down like Winnie the pooh
But if I touch the one down there
That hides beneath your curly hair
After teasing you for an endless hour
It's then I hear your Tigger RAWRRR

{bonus poem 131;-}

Madam Lark of Night

Sweet Madam Lark of Night
What pleasures may I bring you?
What sensations satisfy your desire?
Why does only my pain ignite your fire?

Oh Mistress Philomela
Why do these tears please you so?
While the passions pouring on the floor
From between the beats of my fractured heart

My raptor nightingale
Your talons tare pleasure's howls
Deep through my back out of my grinding teeth
Collapsing to my begging, bloodied knees

{bonus poem 132;-}

Scratch Your Mark on My Tree

I gaze upon your pearl white skin
As you lay yourself down exposed to me
Opening your gate with an invitation of smiles
A kiss through the air brings your lips closer
Closer I stretch mine to your fluff covered nest
The taste of your glaze just inches away
Your scent fills my head as my nose caresses your flesh
While my fingers dance around your button of love
Running them through your sexy curled hair
My tongue reaching out to meet your moist lips
Your hips pushing closer to feed the flames you inspire
A storm of thunder and lightning bursts in the air
Shaking the darkness with electricity's sound
The motion now sways in tune with your moans
Nourishing me with your flowing nectar
Let your sweet honey rain down o'er me
Spraying your fountain of liquid colors
With the release of your rainbow
Drowning my throbbing desire
You explode with a glow

{bonus poem 133}

Dolphins Song

dolphins call across the ocean waves
searching for lovers gone adrift
searching for others left behind in murky waters
that will never reveal the current flowing ever away
and yet it seems all other currents
speed from the vortex swirling all around
never realizing the seas fill in behind from fresh water rivers
while the blinders of broken hearts
create pockets of loneliness even in water
as deep as mountains that fall to the ocean floor
where volcanos vomit blood and steam that turn paradise to Hell
and when they crawled up onto the land to escape their pain
it followed them like a slimey blob of parasites
that grew legs just to remind us that love is as fleeting
as the echoes of our songs that get drowned out
in the plague of sound
we once relied on to bring us back together
when we separated in the past
and now we can't remember the sound of our love song
when we called out to each other
the harmony is split into solo voices off key and out of sync

{bonus poem 134}

Blue Horizons Bleed Red Mist

Wish I could fly my way to Mars
Escape the gravity of reality
And the hopeless blue of skies and seas
Pushing down and drowning me
The heavens glow with points of light
Calling minds too weak to learn
The stars that shower down hold no magic
To make wishes on or guide lost souls
To secret destinations on distant worlds
Where tears are recycled to quench the thirst
Of lips that long for a kiss to wet them instead
For the salty taste of one's own tears
Inspires the craving for more tears to fall
And who am I to reject the truth I can't deny
That like the stars spread across the endless sky
Loneliness is my infinite destiny?

{bonus poem 135}

Dripping Into Death

She looks deeply into my eyes
from behind the veil of sanity
as every inch of her injection
pulls me out of myself
I cannot feel my hands and feet
and my mind is going numb
Moments ago this nurse was not so pretty
as she keeps pushing her finger closer to the end
I am dropping to the floor, dripping into death
My body is excaping me and it's scarring me to life
Though the pain drifts away with the essense of myself
I want to get it back to feel the missing part of me
Soon I will be gone when the injection is complete
And the morphine mingles with the blood inside my brain
While I am seeping into the abyss
I tell her that I don't want to feel like this
But she continues on,
her face as morbid as the thought of what I am becoming
and her smile is reassuring while reeking of evil
as the pain fades with my ability to control my my breath
I ask her three times, is my heart beating in my chest
I don't feel anything, not even alive or dead
I just lay here, assuming I am still laying here
When my back can no longer feel the bed beneath my head
Is this how it feels to journey to Hell once life is lost
Or is this all in my mind to imagine I am melting wax

{bonus poem 136}

After Birth

When did you become so cold your breath hurt
Burning words left me face down in the dirt
And the smile you flashed exposed darker lies
Foreshadowing Hades depth on the rise

Was it your intention to mislead me
When you told me you loved my poetry?
Or did you mean that I should hit the road
And read my love poems far from your abode?

What's the point in going if you stay here
With no one to protect me from my fear?
Poised in the mirror posing as my muse
While the others all agree to refuse

Creeping darkness came to brighten the night
When I thought you inspired me to write
I needed to believe more than to know
The truth was, you just wanted me to go

Where could I go that's far enough away?
How long would be long enough, did you say?
Did you say my dog day would come along
Or did you mean I always had it wrong?

Nine months after reading at the cafe
An icy breeze passed under the doorway
Reborn soon after putting on the show
Cut the cord, now it's time for me to go

{bonus poem 137}

Goodbye

She demanded
Hang up the phone!
Let go of the chord
stretched out between us
Let the connection be lost over the line
That has been crossed more often than you want to know
Say goodbye and press end one last time
There is no one on this end of the call
You placed so long ago you can't remember the sound
That once made your heart race and your ears vibrate
Pulsing with the beat she tapped into your mind
The look in her eyes when she lay next to you
A distant memory that lingers in the darkness
When all there was left to say was goodbye
And you could not bring the words up through your throat
And you could not hang up to hear her voice no more
Her final act was to cut the line like she did your throat
That would not let you speak the words she begged you to say
So now forever in your mind her last word echos, goodbye

{bonus poem 138}

Goodbye Drips from Your Lips

How can I explain without offending you?
I want to be alone in a place you will not go
Somewhere you cannot see or hear me
I just want you as far away from me as possible
So long as I suffer the life I experience
Inside
I feel as though I will soon explode
And I don't want you to get caught in the fall-out
Of my demise, and the icicles that fall from my sky
That I was holding in dungeons dug deep
To keep hidden what I was forbidden to expose
That I had no power to conceal when speaking to your eyes
Or typing softly in your ear what you did not want to hear
Once or twice or fifteen times in your silent absence
I am always alone surrounded by cold cement walls
With windows too high to see outside
Under dripping storm-pipes where water pools
Like tears of sorrow that fall from eyes that cannot see
The smile that never embraces your exquisite lips
While words that burst like fireworks
Make their way through my dying brain
Where they also die in sparkling darkness
As gray becomes black so bright it burns your breath
Each time you speak of what I can never feel
And the movement I see dancing on your lips
Is merely my imagination hoping to witness you smile
A gift I would give you if it cost me my mind
But instead I saw them whisper to my eyes, "goodbye"

{bonus poem 139}

Rusted Rainbows

Another trip to nowhere
Falling Down the same old steps
Taken then taken for a fool
Sold for artificial feelings
And broken like the promises I regret
There isn't a place I can hide
From myself or your memory
There isn't a thought I can conjure
In my aching mess of grey
That will change the stupidity it contains
Even when I thought that I was smart
My brilliance was just a reflection
Of the light you sparkled onto me
Now the rust creeps from my bleeding wounds
Where the sting of your bite lingers
Like fire beneath the veil of sin cast over me
Alone like the groundhog predicted I would be
Repeating like the chucking away of the days
In a pile of wood dried for burning beneath my corpse
Apologies won't bring back the life that was lost
Driving stakes into the heart of the bloodsucking fool
As the bonfire rages through the caverns of my heart
Boiling the red liquid that cooks me from the inside out
Like unholy water from the river Styx
That simmers in anticipation of my arrival
My paralysis binds my arms from reaching out to you
But then you wouldn't save me from sinking any deeper
And I don't deserve to be redeemed by an angel anyway
So what's the point in begging when there's no food on the table?
Just light the flame of my crumbling pyre and let it be done
And set my ashes free over the waterfalls I long to wash over me
In the mist of the water that sprays from underneath
A rainbow sparkles in the sunlight where I look out
To see you waiving goodbye to me

{bonus poem 140}

How?

How can I read your words of desire
when I know they are not for me?
How can I see them
when the muse who inspires you absorbs your moonlight?
I cannot
I cannot

How can I write the words in my heart
into words that will touch your soul?
How can I tell you of my desire
to be the one you inspire to write love poetry?
I cannot
I cannot

How can I see in the dark
when storm clouds cover the moon after midnight?
How can I breathe
when tornados rage while sucking the wind out of me?
I cannot
I cannot

How can I sleep
when the thunder I hear is the banging of your bed without me?
How can I wake when the dawn will not break
before the heart that is falling apart?
I cannot
I cannot

{bonus poem 141}

Jealousy is Such a Bitch

Nowhere feels like home and this home is only walls with a roof
Threads that stretch into the past are frayed and flutter in the breeze
Blowing from a drafty dark corridor that smells of decaying dreams
Or is it my dirty laundry i keep hidden in cloak rooms and trash bags
Hoping no one notices the dust covering
the stories i polished with lies
Or the lies i painted to distract you from the truth i never told
About the jealousy that rages within me for the love i cannot have
Because you give it to a pig undeserving of your heart
As my lips form the word
but my voice cannot speak its sound
Bitch!
You are all that word implies and very little more
Though you pretend to be an angel, you have fallen to your knees
And like all fallen angels you are bound to go to Hell
I would leave here if i had somewhere to go
But another home would be no more familiar
than this empty bunch of walls
With a roof that cannot protect me from the cold you exude
That lingers in the air with the scent of your rotting corpse
in my laundry bags
Besides, i am tired of dragging you around with me
from one roof to another
I wonder, are you happy now?
Are you getting that deep tan you always wished for?
It can't be hotter than Hell in Hades
but I can still hear you bitching that it's so

{bonus poem 142}

Masturbating Reminds Me I am

Endorphins frantically race through my brain
Fooling my heart to feel no more pain
A rush of blood to flood these imprisoned cells
Rising higher and deeper with each lie that it tells
Of beautiful lovers and others without faces
Covering me in scars but leaving no traces
When orgasmic storms wash over head
Thunderous warnings mock each word that she said
Her hand slips away revealing her fingers are mine
In darkness reality crosses a forbidden line
There is an uneasy calm after the cumming has gone
When all that remains is a lonely sad song
No one is here to hold me and care
My cock has gone soft and I can't breathe this air
Washing reminds me that nothing is free
The cost of pretending was my sanity

{bonus poem 143}

Nobody Knows the Trouble I've Sown

Nobody knows the trouble I've sown
Nobody sees darkness in one so alone
Will I be forgiven if her heart turns to stone?
Or will I die lonely and buried unknown?

Oh No! Death
Don't come for me now
Before I end up six feet under the ground
My soul needs forgiveness before I lay down
Where eternities waiting to make ashes of me
Oh No! Death, I'm not ready to descend below
While she still has the power to set my soul free

Nobody knows but Jes's
Nobody knows the sorrow I feel
For the love I pretended that never was real
Please allow me the last word to pray my appeal

Nobody knows me or what I have done
Nobody but Jes's
Can cut the rope from my tree
But Lord, Jes's won't ever forgive my lustful dark sins
For a call that I made she'll never forgive me
Unless the risen son enlightens the dawn

Oh No! Death
Please allow me one final breath
To find redemption
To beg Lord Jes's down on my knees
In my final confession
Where the truth cannot freeze

Oh No! Death
Don't touch me until the words are spoken
Grant me a pardon from her poetic pen
Stay the sentence of "death"
Else every memory of me will be destroyed
With my forgotten lost soul declared Null and Void

{bonus poem 144}

Death-right

I live in fear of the future
Because soon enough I won't be in it
Alone in life is only one step away from nothing
Will anyone notice when I am gone?
Will anyone miss the look in my eyes?
When ears can no longer hear the sound of my voice
My words reach out in silence
from the pages of books unopened
Is there anyone there to care or remember my heart?
Or will I be as forgotten as the children I never had?
My DNA will die with me
No one longs to pass on
The debt of life to generations alive in my imagination
If only, if only, if only
But the echo of only is distorted into lonely
While no gravestone marks a plot of land
To speak my name to passersby of when I was alive
Just pages in two books of poetry
That cry-out to the eyes
Of curious minds who stumble
Across a few dozen copies left lying around
Discarded by some, shelved by others
Perhaps a hundred years from now, someone will find one
Maybe my words will be read again in the future
That I fear because I will not be there
And no one will care

There is Someone Deeper than Dark

Deeper than the flesh
Deeper than dark blood
At depths where even bone feels alone
Where secrets go to remain unknown
Existing between the heart and the light
Trapped beneath the gravity of life
That swollows hope and spits out love
That leaves a twisted sense of direction
Confusing your face with no reflection
Futile attemps to cut through stained wood
To the portal keeping you from womanhood
No virgin blood will lubricate a path love does not illuminate
Far deeper than the swords of molesters penetrate
Deeper, dig deeper to where razors cannot slice
There is somewhere you have always been
Deeper than doctors and poets have seen
In you there is someone waiting to break free
From behind the eyes afraid to see
The shortest distance between here and there
Is the step untaken to nowhere
Through a doorway you're holding the key for
Holding in a past that isn't needed anymore
There is nowhere for the one you lost to run and hide
There is somewhere deeper to release the pain still loose inside

{bonus poem 146}

Secret Sins

She floats like a dark radiant mist
Above and around me she prowls
Although I cannot see her
I know that she is there
I sense her gaze upon my flesh
Peering through her gown of mesh
Sewn of thread died black in ancient darkness
Collecting secrets of the unsuspecting souls
Who waltz past her shadow, secure within their thoughts
Unhidden from her eyes as they whisper in her ears
Their most intimate thoughts and cherished desires
And worst of all their deepest fears
Her fate to reveal them is woven into the tapestry of her soul
There is nothing that she will not know
Or reveal in dreams when her dark winds blow
Stealing lust from each man that she desires
Who rarely feel her coming or see her going
Amid their smoldering after-fires
Sensing they have been had and yet unknowing
The craft that carries her away knows the course that she must follow
Leading her from heart to heart as she infects their sleeping souls
Awakening their bodies while their minds are deep asleep
Harvesting their passions like the secrets that she keeps
She was born to Captain her drifting sea-less ship
To see more truth in darkness than exposed in light of day
For there are more lies in lustful minds
Than truths they ever told
And now she tells the tales she steals
While replacing them with lustful dreams
That smell so real it burns and feels
Unlike the hands of the one now sleeping in their arms
As the moist and fragrant drops linger on his loins
He is unsure if more than thoughts were stolen
By a dark shadow lover touched yet never seen
His arm embraces a woman that must never hear
The howling sounds of her passionate winds
He was haunted by in the dark of night
He prays she never learns of his secret sins

{bonus poem 147}

Between Reality and Hell

I did not know I am not real
Tricked my mind into believing
A life had something to do with having a heart
Beating somewhere between Heaven and Hell
That felt an imaginary emotion someone dubbed love
To write greeting cards that said what love is
Without having a clue how it felt to fall into its pit
But what does it matter?
It's just pretend and I am not real
A whisper from the fantasies of trees where birds nest
And bees live to pollinate the fruit that grows on their branches
Being at the whim of the fantasies of creatures that fly
While I am left standing on the ground that seems as real as me
I wonder if I will fade away into the space I do not really occupy
When flames come to burn the tree into ashes
and kill the winged life-bringers
When they are gone who will there be to keep imagining me?
Who will there be to mourn my passing
into the nothingness from which I sprang?
How could I know I was not real
when I touched the leaves that left each fall?
Each fall when I thought what I felt was love, but was nothing more
Than the birds and bees in their battle to control the tree
To control the other who each depended on and saw as an enemy
Instead of looking on each other as lovers with a real destiny
But the fruit was there to tempt them and tell them lies
And I was born from the indigestion of birds who ate bees
And bees who helped the fruit multiply for humans to be tempted by
So I, the first man, was tempted and became unreal as the fire came
And the birds saw, and the bees saw and they were sad
And they knew that it was not good
So the birds sang and the bees buzzed and I became ashes
And to ashes I have fallen time and time again
From the fantasies of birds and bees who pretend to be lovers

{bonus poem 148}

Hiding Hollow Eyes

She lives in a fantasy world
dreaming from within her pretend life
She told me I was the one
to be the father and she would be the wife
She fell asleep where the weaver wove
a dream of silk and softer skies
She lost her way and forgot my name
then turned away to hide her hollow eyes

I wanted so badly to believe this love
was more than mere fleeting dreams
I was willing to close my eyes
let the weaver sew me in between the seems
I would have made children with her
and been her San Franciscan Knight
I told her you can't turn left there
but that don't matter 'cos everything's alright

The hidden trouble was,
not a word from her was true and she never knew
The story in her was written
while she slept between breezes that never blew
The love she tried to give was a fever
escaping her pores in droplets of passionate sweat
The future we planned was all in the mind
of the wanton lover that I never met

Is he rich enough to recover
from the drain all your sucking will do to his wealth?
Is he young enough to discover
new love after he finds all was stolen using stealth?
Is he wise enough to realize
that before he's dead all his dreams have got to go?
Is he strong enough to take
the crushing blow when he learns all he don't really know?

{bonus poem 149}

Myst-air-E-girl

She wasn't even real
After all I promised her
She was nothing more than an Email
That responded with gestures of sex
Then vanished into thin air
Leaving behind a scented mist that hung like clouds
Darkening my eyes with false passion
And teasing my throbbing muscle
That bangs within my chest
Wanting more of the never ending pain
Than of the silent peace she has left behind
Denied the taste of her sensual puffy lips
When all that remains is a fantasy
And a question that no answer will ever satisfy
Was she even a real woman or just a auto-responding bot
An electronic artist that colored my eyes with shades of gray
And drops of sweat that trickled down my thighs
Moistening my desire with mental nudity
I would have shared my everything and every thing
If only she were flesh and blood and poetry
If only she were as real as me
She could be my poetry
Now she is lines of white-out across my page
A mistake I can't erase that leaves paper scars
Like stitches in the skin my chest can't heal
Forever marked by the look her eyes etched into me
I wish I could forget her like old memories
Because being alone fucking sucks
And I hate being fooled and made a fool
And god damn I hate being old!

{bonus poem 150}

I Remember When

I thought you were interesting
Thought your poetry was so deep and sensual
Thought you had as much mind between your ears
As bush between your legs
When you knew I thought it was the sexiest damned thing
Warm and womanly like your momma-toos
From the baby that stretched your tummy
Leaving behind your tiger stripes
But lke all the rest of the plastic personality
That used to look so cool on you
The darkness you put on for show
Has taken your talent to the toilet
And flushed your art away
Into a gutter of dirt and disparaging remarks
About a man who loved you and would have given everything
To be a part of your color-filled world of creativity
Until you turned it into shades of gray and Smokey haze
I remember when
I thought you were beautiful
Ahh, but I was just a fool

{bonus poem 151}

Nothing Is Real

Plastic faces drifting past me
Their eyes painted on to pretend they can see
Always looking up with their heads facing down
Layers of make-up smeared into the smile of a clown
Never showing anything but their molded reflection
Picked out in the mirror from an on-line selection
I'm tired of that look and their soulless stare
The only thing more stagnate is that god awful hair
It's a world of walking mannequins pretending life cannot win
Hiding themselves under plaster for skin
Am I the last one left to see the masks we've put on?
The only one left to laugh at the joke we've become?
I feel alone on crowded streets and when I'm at home
Time to put on my mask and become a lawn gnome

{bonus poem 152}

afraid

There are so many things that suck about living life alone
The loneliness is obvious, Nighttime is the worst
Not just for the empty space next to me in bed
Not just for the heart that never beats against my chest
But when I try to fall asleep the phantoms come to me
And if they take me in my sleep no one will know I've ceased to be
Weeks could go by but for the smell of my lifeless rotting corpse
Or as my fluid leftovers seep through the boards
down to the bar beneath me
into the drinks of drunks who might wonder
what's the extra in their glass?
Until someone spots me pooling up on the barroom floor
And then looks up to see me dripping down on them
Right in the eye of the guy who keeps playing the dam jukebox
Night after night with the same dam songs I've come to hate
Maybe I can spill some of my guts into that box
To short out the power and burn the building down to the ground
Until that time I am up here dying by myself with no one else
No one knows how it feels to be alone for twenty-four years
The word loneliness died so long ago
I can't remember how good it used to feel
And whatever this emptiness has become inside my twisted tree
Now makes me long for the nights when I could cry myself to sleep
At least I knew that I was alive as ghosts do not shed tears
For so long there's been no one here laying next to me
Waking up to sunlight next to my breathless, still cold body
When the night before I was so warm and loving as she slept
Inside of my embrace until the morning when she wept
So I guess it's for the best to pass away and be unmourned
Then be reborn a mass of gelatin
in the drinks of drunks who taste loneliness
at the bottom of each glass they down
Until at last their sorrows drown

{bonus poem 153}

A Hero's Secret

Hiding the secret
Behind capes and cowls and lies
From everyone who admires you
When the disguise fits so perfectly
The super hero becomes his burden
A barrier between reality and make believe
Justifying the crimes of vigilantism
With arrogance that witnesses birthing legends
While the one locked behind a tattered veil
Forms a prison within the flesh of his reflection
Altered by his ego behind a mirror he longs to smash
Knowing that breaking the glass could shatter
The dreams of falling in love to conceive confidence
From the trials of self-authored crucibles
Seeking justice in his personal conviction
That somehow he saved the ones who looked up
Into his mirror mounted on an invisible cloud
Waiting for Lucy to reveal her ugly head
Waiting for each piece to take its place
To alleviate its own relentless loneliness
Crowded by empty, suffocating lost souls
Allowing her arch enemy to believe his secret is safe

{bonus poem 134;-}

T-1-2

Three wheels touched down to a rugged skidding sound
Their jets delivered more dreams than bulging baggage
To a place where dreams rise to heights above the sky
Two souls await their physical forms to follow
They step off the ramp and into each other's hearts
Taxi cab driver awaits his passengers stepping off the taxied jets
Taking both to a long awaited destination
Trembling with an ancient anticipation
Tickling them within as nerves crackle with desire
That consumes their naked bodies beneath layers of warm clothing
Tempting them to tear off the fibers torturing their skin
Teasing their flesh with covered caresses and hidden hardness's
Tasting long desired lips for the first time, for so long
Time seems to stand still as feet inch closer together
Together for the first time but still too far apart
Tying arms together in an embrace long overdue
Touching skin to skin from nose to toes
Tethered in the center by their sensual bond
Tackling each other onto a bed of pure delight
Tracing each other's curves exposed in ecstasy
Tongues tasting tasty places
Till the trembling shakes the foundation of their dreams
Trashing all pretense with the reality of love
Truth unfolds the future, revealing for them both
Telling tales of blissful fantasies come true
Then making way for making love
The way new lovers do
Tonight as the unlikely pair unite
Talking of this moment was never quite like this
This moment in time and space with no space left in between
These souls flew a mile high to reach their destiny
Towards perpetual love for one eternity

{bonus poem 155}

The Outline of My Lover

I used to dream in black and white but now I dream in color
It used to be that every cloud hid it's silver lining behind shadows
But now even the darkest of clouds expose the outline of my lover
While pain has died in a silver noose that dangles from my gallows

I have waited all my life for a light to shine
where none had ever shown
To warm my heart by a fireplace glowing from the embers of my soul
They'd grown so cold I was sure
that I had not learned all that I've known
That snow flakes on my heart concealed
nothing more than an empty hole

I was lonely in ways that fooled the fools who never knew me
And the ones who did could not see the cloud that had no lining
For hidden inside me was a man who could not set the darkness free
Embracing emptiness to form delusion's fog of grand designing

At first you tried to shatter myths I had molded into gods
Who would not show the silver that could expose you as my other
Till darkness painted a rainbow from gold blinding my demigods
In lonely times I dreamt in black and white but now I dream in color

{bonus poem 156}

To One Too Alone - Two Alone Too Bad

Why didn't you tell me
You had feelings deep within your heart?
Hoping I would ask you
To hook up and never fall apart
I would have jumped right in
I would have loved to sink and swim
I would have given you anything
And shared your every sin

Why didn't you tell me
You allowed me in your broken mind?
Hoping I would fix it
And glue each cracked shell fragment into place
I could not see it in your eyes
I could not imagine to realize
I never heard it in your soft blue voice
I never knew I was your only choice
And never got to see your smile

Why didn't you tell me?
You wanted me to take the task
To bare your burdens and be the cask
For all the shattered dreams and broken promises
And the smiles you wore behind your frowning mask
Cos it's just cooler to express unfeeling grimaces
Than to let me see a face that wasn't made of wax
Too late I see with clarity the question I must ask
Why didn't I tell you?

Mae I Call You Juliet? {bonus poem 157}

When last we spoke I asked "Mae I call you Juliet?"
Reaching out to touch your digits I promised never to forget
Your despair became more real with each poem that I read
And when your pain stopped flowing I feared your heart was dead
The only thing you couldn't hide behind
Was the painted smile that I saw through over your invisible disguise
Pouring out the memories with every teardrop that you've shed
A crimson pillow case can't conceal all the times your heart has bled
When the truth in each other's eyes hides behind a clear disguise
Two voices cannot speak within ears silent to hear
Lost hearts do not beat in harmony
with the clicking of keys on boards
In quite the same way as when fingers play scales
up and down naked spines or quivering cut thighs...
The only thing you couldn't hold inside
Was the red that kept your heart alive
Your ghost now haunts my thoughts even though you're still alive
Some say suicide is painless but no one has died and lived to tell
So much pain to follow you to Hell
and one can ever know what dreams may come after we go
My bottle's full of pills to take away my pain
Beyond thunder storms of tears hidden by the rain
Falling like angels on a Hell bound crazy train
Chain your heart to a dream you'll never share
And shackle yourself in the dungeon of despair
So long as you believe that life is never fair
Clinging to a master who needs you not, nor does he care
Every shadow is born from a light on the other side of somewhere
The beauty in you casts a shadow made of light
Blinding bolts reflecting off the dark midnight
Unseen by souls that lost their mortal fight
Showered in ambient shadows to hasten their loss of sight
But even here where black is bright
I know that you see me, do you know that I see you?
Can you see unbound unconditional love
Offers equal opportunity unity?

{bonus poem 158}

Nothing Before Me, Nothing Behind

At daybreak I woke from a dread-filled dark dream
Opening my eyes to infinite nothing
Feeling my way to the light switch on my wall
The sound of the click was momentary relief
As the glow of the bulb revealed more darkness to me
Than I had ever seen before or behind
A blanket of black entrapped the shape of my hands
Cloaking the image in the mirror that looked back at me
With eyes as wide open as my own though lacking perception
Sensing motion in darkness, seeing waves of cold wind
Carrying smoke so thick it choked my thoughts dry
Till I could not quench this thirst
with all of the tears from each eye
Cried in blindness in a mind without light
Without a glimmer of hope or a shadow of white
What terrible curse has stolen a visionaries' site?
Turning the morning's sunrise into an endless midnight
Even my once vivid memory of your beautiful face
Has faded to shackles of black leather and lace
Blindfolds of satin appear covering these eyes
Clearly this dream became a nightmare of lies
Where rainbows once rose to shower on me
Now vacant your once sparkling gaze
In a mind full of one color
There is nothing to see

{bonus poem 159}

Ghosts

Flashes of recall strike at my thoughts
Thunderous echoes of faces forgotten
Shimmer in the back of my clouded mind
They could be from reveries or lost moments of time
I don't know if I knew them or imagined we met
I may have made love to the ghosts I can’t see
In brief glimpses of passion that might have been fantasy
I can't tell if they're real or can remember me
Still I long to merge spirits with vaporous phantoms
Share corporal warmth, kiss sweat covered skin
What is the difference between veracity and erratic dreams
When the lines have broken as gray swirls in my skull
No boundaries exist to separate humidity from mist
And I feel so lost and alone within my own mind
Imagined vague figments who loved like lightening at night
Now haunt the dark hallways of black holes in my brain
Sucked into the void of my dead memory
I hear their tears dripping to moisten my head

{bonus poem 160}

Passion and Pain

They're not just some words to be stolen
But the meter beating within my heart
On the pages of my passion
Spilled while the wounds were still left open
In black and white and deepest red bled the colors of my art
So it's not surprising you can't understand
Your claim upon my imagery is creative thievery
While your sleight of hand reveals your warped dishonesty
You shout imitation is the sincerest form of flattery
But if that is true why wear a mask to conceal your robbery
It's not enough to later say you admire my painted words
Writing means much more to me
than flushing defecated words
They are all I have experienced in passion and in pain
They are everything that healed my mind
and all that kept me sane
We may share all of our feelings in similar shades of ink
But my poems ownership still belongs to me
Yet through all of that you can still borrow my verse
Each time you read my poetry

www.ingramcontent.com/pod-product-compliance
Lightning Source LLC
LaVergne TN
LVHW011228080426
835509LV00005B/380

* 9 7 8 0 6 1 5 5 0 3 9 4 3 *